A PASSION FOR PLACES

ENGLAND THROUGH THE EYES OF JOHN BETJEMAN

DAVID MEARA

AMBERLEY

St Enodoc, Trebetherick, Cornwall. The little church nestling among the sand dunes where John Betjeman is buried, near to the graves of his parents, was one of his favourite churches. (Courtesy of Stuart Vallis)

Lord, I have loved the habitation of thy house, and the place where thine honour dwelleth.

(Psalm 26:8)

To Gordon and Richard: good friends and fellow church crawlers

First published 2021

Amberley Publishing
The Hill, Stroud,
Gloucestershire, GL5 4EP

www.amberley-books.com

ISBN: 978 1 4456 8710 0 (print)
ISBN: 978 1 4456 8711 7 (ebook)

British Library Cataloguing in Publication Data.
A catalogue record for this book is available from the British Library.

Typeset in 10pt on 13pt Celeste.
Typesetting by SJmagic DESIGN SERVICES, India.
Printed in the UK.

Contents

Foreword by Sir Simon Jenkins FSA FRSL, Author of *England's Thousand Best Churches*

John Betjeman was always accessible. I first heard him at a lecture in Oxford when I was an undergraduate. His topic was aesthetics and his text the remark of a woman who had said to him, 'Oh Mr Betjeman, I've just seen an absolutely hideous building; I know you would love it.' This paradox of beauty instantly appealed to me. Five years later he summoned me to his Chelsea home to ask for help in saving an electricity sub-station in Mayfair. I failed initially to see its charm, but by the time I left, I was a convert. The Duke Street sub-station survives to this day.

For the rest of Betjeman's life, I regularly accompanied him on wanderings round London and its suburbs. We visited variously St Paul's, Baker Street, Southwark, Edgware, Covent Garden, Metro-land, Southend, Broad Street station and churches galore. On them all he showered an indiscriminate affection. He loved buildings by personifying them, by imagining them arm in arm with those who used them. To Ruskin, for a thousand who could think, only one could see. Betjeman could see. I am sure it mattered that he was

Sir John Betjeman (1906–84) with Archie and Jumbo, his treasured childhood soft toys, who accompanied him throughout his life. Although he had an infectious laugh and was excellent company, he could also look pensive or melancholy, a sign of the depressive streak that lay just below the surface. (Courtesy of Jonathan Stedall)

self-taught. To learn properly we must be led by our instincts, not the doctrine of others. That was for the Pevsners of this world.

I would compare Betjeman with my other early hero, Alex Clifton-Taylor. On approaching a building, Clifton-Taylor would act the geologist, sensing the ground and inspecting every stone as with a magnifying glass. Betjeman would approach as a supplicant, throwing up his arms, gasping with delight, addressing imaginary (and sometimes real) bystanders. He dressed materials in emotion and nostalgia. He would adorn them if possible with a touch of humour. On our epic circumnavigation of the churches of Heathrow, he cackled with

John Betjeman wanted people to start looking properly and carefully at their surroundings, and himself possessed a 'seeing eye'. In the John Betjeman Centre in Wadebridge, Cornwall, are his spectacles, through which he looked *at* things, instead of just through them. And then, as he said, 'Life starts absolutely crackling with interest and excitement.' (Courtesy of Stuart Vallis)

Looking over Port Isaac, Cornwall. This picturesque fishing village, with narrow lanes, old slate-hung houses and an inn on the harbour's edge, was a favourite haunt of John Betjeman's, who is still remembered by the older inhabitants. (Courtesy of Stuart Vallis)

laughter as each ghastly philistine plane roared overhead, exulting in the brief moment of ecclesiastical calm that followed. If a new runway is built at Heathrow, I dream of Betjeman's Harmondsworth church, reincarnated as its first-class lounge.

As an atheist I saw churches as treasure troves of art and history, rather than manifestations of faith. But Betjeman, himself haunted by 'doubts', made me see significance in what they meant for others. At his memorial service, Harry Williams spoke of his awareness of mystery. To Betjeman a church was a spirit of place left unresolved, mystery hovering in air, a miasma of personal memories and hesitant beliefs. This was why he found the Anglo-Catholic liturgy so comforting. It gave substance to mystery.

At odds with a modernism which, for so much of his life, had disparaged and ridiculed him, Betjeman found solace in the past, in all its guises. But he craved for it present-day reference, which was why he hurled himself at the emergent conservation movement. He was therefore delighted to discover, in the 1970s, a growing band of young sympathisers ready to worship at his feet.

Most of the battles of that time – St Pancras, Covent Garden, Somerset House, Broad Street station, the Coal Exchange, St Mary-at-Hill – had Betjeman as their inspiration. Most, not all, were won. Stations were no longer demolished. The beloved Edwardians were recognized as the last great stylists. Lyrical parody was never far from Betjeman's lips. Faced with a faintly tedious Covent Garden façade, he murmured, 'Could it be, could it be, early Maufe?'

Betjeman's most enjoyable legacy is to lend himself so readily to exegesis, as David Meara's book shows. He was a poet of his age and station and a gloriously photogenic performer. But when it came to architecture, his contribution came at a crucial turning point. In the 1960s and '70s, a Britain seized by official modernism was truly on the brink of demolishing the bulk of its architectural heritage. Through his eye and his pen, Betjeman championed those who were to forestal this disaster. He was truly a warrior poet.

Acknowledgements

This book has been a labour of love on my part, but many people have given it a helping hand along the way. It is the illustrations that really bring a book like this to life, and I am particularly grateful to Stuart Vallis for travelling around the country with me and taking many of the photographs. I would also like to thank the Tate Gallery Archive, the Historic England Photographic Archive, the London Metropolitan Archive and Islington Local History Centre, Alamy Stock Images, Christina Hemmett at the Athenaeum, the clerk William Alden and Ruxandra Oprea at the Worshipful Company of Stationers and Newspaper Makers, the Country Life Picture Library, and Ann Wickham and Father Marcus Walker for their help in sourcing many of the images. I would like to thank the trustees of the estate of John Piper, and Jeremy Smith and the estate of Geoffrey Fletcher, for permission to use their material. Also Karen at the Tom Brown's School Museum at Uffington, Richard Ingrams, Jonathan Stedall, Gordon Mursell, Simon Jenkins and George Middleton for help and advice when conducting the research for this book. Stewart Roach and Melinda Cole gave valuable technical help and Tracey Salt typed and retyped the manuscript, and my heartfelt thanks go to them. I have relied heavily on those who have already written extensively about John Betjeman, especially Bevis Hillier, Candida Lycett Green, Kevin Gardner, Stephen Games, A. N. Wilson and William Peterson, and owe them a great debt for their many insights.

I have endeavoured to contact the copyright holders of the images, drawings and paintings I have used as illustrations in this book, but in case of oversight please contact me so that future acknowledgement can be made.

Lastly, I would like to thank Rosemary, my wife, for her patience, support and encouragement, which have kept me going and made the whole enterprise such a pleasure. I would also like to express the debt I owe to John Betjeman himself, whose writings and TV programmes fanned the flames of my juvenile enthusiasm and encouraged me to open my eyes to the buildings and landscapes that have been an abiding interest and passion ever since.

Introduction

On St Peter's Day, Friday 29 June 1984, if you had happened to be passing through Broad Sanctuary in Westminster in the middle of the morning you would have noticed large numbers of people queuing to enter Westminster Abbey, with police in attendance and extra security in place. The occasion was the memorial service for the Poet Laureate Sir John Betjeman, attended not just by his family and friends, but by figures from the arts, the theatre, politics, the Church of England and members of the royal family, including the Prince of Wales, Princess Margaret, the Duke of Gloucester and representatives of HM the Queen. Thus the 'great and the good' mingled with hundreds of members of the public who had come to pay their respects to a poet and writer who had chronicled and celebrated the ordinary and the everyday and made them look afresh at their surroundings. I, too, was among the 2,000 people who gathered that day to give thanks for a man who, in the Dean of Westminster's words, had 'cast an aura of romance and nostalgia over ordinary and familiar things', and who first kindled in me a love of church buildings, railways and Victorian architecture. It was an extraordinary and moving occasion when the writer who had been dismissed as a joker in the 1930s, ridiculed as a poet by modernist critics in the 1950s, and looked down on as a lightweight television performer in the 1960s and '70s finally achieved his apotheosis as a national treasure who had moulded a nation's taste and touched millions with his poetry, writing, campaigning and television work.

John Betjeman had always been a prey to self-doubt, troubled by 'imposter syndrome' and fearful of being found out. Such insecurity made him easily jealous or offended and prone to bear lifelong grudges. However, behind the brittle exterior there was an inner warmth of heart, and a sureness of touch kindled both by his conviction that writing poetry was his vocation and by a strong visual awareness that made him curious about people, buildings and places, and eager to communicate that enthusiasm to others. In chapter two of his verse autobiography *Summoned by Bells* Betjeman wrote:

> For myself I knew as soon as I could read and write
> That I must be a poet...

'Calling out to me for words...' Daymer Bay, Trebetherick, Cornwall. (Courtesy of Stuart Vallis)

That word 'poet' denotes not just a writer of verses, but someone who approaches life in a particular way, who looks beyond the surface of things and discovers hidden mystery and meaning in the ordinary and the everyday. In the same chapter he goes on to say that Atlantic rollers, 'church bells, and the puff of trains, the sight of sailing clouds, the smell of grass – were always calling out to me for words'. His sense that 'awe and mystery were everywhere' was an essential part of his poetic impulse, his love of the built environment and above all the men and women who peopled it. He wrote in one of his letters to John Sparrow in December 1947: 'I am not primarily a poet of place. I never write of place first and people afterwards (at least not nowadays), but of people first and place as an inextricable part of them.'

Betjeman's great friend and confidant Harry Williams, who was to become Dean of Trinity College Cambridge and who gave the address at his memorial service, had expressed some years earlier in a sermon what John Betjeman had felt deeply all his life:

The one thing necessary is to be open and prepared for mystery; to understand that familiar things are not just or only familiar things but that they invite us on a voyage of discovery in order to show us a richness, a subtlety, a depth which we formerly never dreamt existed. The one thing necessary I suggest, is at least to be on the look-out for that to happen; it is to be expectant as we live in our ordinary world because the world is not really ordinary at all in the usual sense; it's full of hitherto unforeseen and unimagined wonder. For our world, like all worlds, is a dwelling place

9

of mystery; mystery, remember, is not the same thing as mystification; mystery is not to be abstruse or tortuous or underhand in our thinking, nor is mystery a riddle or enigma which in principle can be solved and which in time will be solved by intellectual effort; that is to say mystery is not what we invoke when science for the time being can tell us no more. Mystery is the atmosphere in which we live if only we could have our eyes open to see it; it glimmers and twinkles all around us and beckons us to communion with itself, and the communion is a felt communion, it's not something which we can intellectually dissect or analyse. Mystery impinges upon us as a presence, an inexhaustible presence, everywhere, in all things, and to be aware of the presence, to be aware of the mystery in all things is not to find those things faded away or melted down; on the contrary, to perceive the mystery in anything is to find it more itself than we ever found it before, because it is in pointing beyond themselves that things are most fully themselves.

The fact that Harry Williams understood that Betjeman not only believed this himself, but embodied it in his writing, is perhaps revealed in the dedication he put in the front of a

Harry Williams CR (1919–2006) with John Betjeman. After an academic career as a priest and theologian, which culminated in being Dean of Trinity College, Cambridge, Harry Williams, aged fifty, became a monk and joined the Community of the Resurrection at Mirfield in Yorkshire. He was an inspiring preacher and published a number of books exploring Christianity from a psychological perspective. He and John Betjeman became great friends, and were photographed together here in 1981. (Courtesy of Jonathan Stedall)

book of his talks about prayer, which he published in 1977. The dedication reads: 'To John Betjeman (because he likes dim things) with love and admiration.'

The book is based on a series of talks about prayer in which Williams states: 'We are all of us in some degree or other alienated from our truest selves. My truest self is the place within me where God dwells. And in prayer I have access to my truest self...' This sometimes painful journey of self-discovery is summed up by the book's title, *Becoming What I Am.* Williams would have known of Betjeman's struggles with faith, doubt and identity through their close friendship, and in dedicating the book to him Williams clearly felt that Betjeman was himself moving towards the acceptance of his own truest self, both publicly and privately.

This is the process that Betjeman describes so candidly in his verse autobiography *Summoned by Bells.* He had been working on this since the early years of the Second World War, and it was finally published in 1960. The title sums up the subject matter, which describes John Betjeman's progress from childhood through his time at Marlborough and Oxford, to his employment as a prep schoolmaster. Behind his description of growing up sound the bells of London and Oxford, and country churches everywhere, calling him both to explore church buildings and to grapple with the 'arduous love affair of faith'. It was a remarkably brave thing to do, to bare his soul in verse in this way, and there were many contemporary voices raised in mockery and criticism. But the book was hugely popular, selling out the first printing of 75,000 copies and then being reprinted, and clearly resonating with the public consciousness. The writer Raymond Mortimer commented, 'We say to ourselves not "This is poetry" but "This is the truth".' Betjeman's fellow poet Philip Larkin defended the poem against its critics and said in words that prefigured Harry Williams's book title: 'The age has accepted him in the most unambiguous way possible: it is really a triumph. Betjeman has made it. He has become Betjeman.'

The publication of *Summoned by Bells* in 1960 in a way set the seal upon the process, begun in his undergraduate days, of blending together his multiple personae in one harmonious whole: the music hall turn, the well-read antiquary, the lover of forgotten buildings, styles and architects, the social networker and climber, the poet, and the radio and television personality. He had become what he truly was and found his unique voice.

Since his death in 1984 his reputation as a poet initially waned, but he is now firmly rehabilitated as an important twentieth-century figure. A number of books have been written about him, most notably Bevis Hillier's magisterial three-volume life, and his letters have been sensitively selected by his daughter Candida Lycett-Green, with a biographical commentary. His prose and broadcast works have been edited and published by Stephen Games, and Kevin Gardner has written perceptively about his Christian faith. So, what more is there to say?

This book is neither a biography, nor a commentary. It is an extended essay that looks at the way John Betjeman understood and interpreted the places and buildings that were so important to him. He told a journalist in 1955: 'If I have a mission, it is to show people things which are beautiful so that they will realise very soon what is ugly. When you look at things, instead of just looking through them, life starts absolutely crackling with interest and excitement.' Throughout his life he nursed a number of personal grudges, notably against his former tutor at Magdalen College, Oxford, the writer and future Christian apologist C. S. Lewis. Although Betjeman loved the life of an undergraduate at Magdalen, living in oak-panelled eighteenth-century rooms in the gracious New Building overlooking

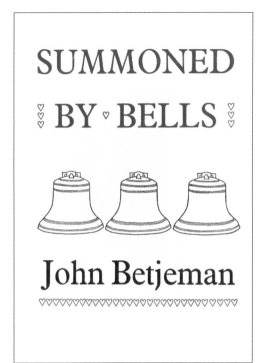

Above left: This autobiography in verse was published in 1960. John Betjeman was particularly exercised about the book jacket, and various designs and colours were suggested, including the use of brown paper, a variation of which was adopted. The endpapers give the effect of bells being rung, the 'bell changes' reading from left to right. The book was printed by William Clowes & Sons Ltd on antique laid paper, with drawings by Michael Tree.

Above right: Founded by William of Waynflete, Bishop of Winchester in 1458, Magdalen College boasts some fine buildings. Magdalen Tower, built by William Orchard between 1492 and 1509, is an imposing landmark on the approach to the city over Magdalen Bridge. John Betjeman came up as an undergraduate in 1925 and had rooms in the eighteenth-century New Building, which looks out on the Deer Park. (Drawing by W. G. Blackall from *The Charm of Oxford* by J. Wells, London, 1920)

the Deer Park, and working hard at what interested him, he was, academically speaking, a failure. He was a committed 'aesthete', not a 'hearty', revelling in charvet silk ties, 'luncheons, luncheons all the way', and outings to stately homes with his aristocratic friends. Sadly, he had the misfortune to have been assigned to the young, bluff Northern Irish tutor C. S. Lewis: tweed-jacketed, pipe smoking, beer drinking and hearty – everything that John Betjeman was not. Lewis took a dislike to the Anglo-Catholic aesthete who admired obscure Victorian poets, was bored by Anglo-Saxon poetry, revelled in the ritual kaleidoscope of the Church of England and often failed to turn up for tutorials. So, when Betjeman twice failed the First Public Examination in Holy Scripture ('Divvers') in his third year, Lewis was unsympathetic and unhelpful. For the rest of his life Betjeman blamed Lewis for not supporting him and thereby banishing him from his Oxford paradise. In a long letter written to Lewis eight years after being sent down he gave vent to his pent-up resentment

Above: Magdalen College, Oxford. The tower that climbs above the trees welcomes the visitor to Oxford and the undergraduate at the beginning of the academic year.

Right: Clive Staples Lewis (1898–1963) was a fellow of Magdalen College, Oxford, and John Betjeman's English tutor. He had served in the First World War and at the time John Betjeman was being taught by him was a declared atheist. The photograph shows Lewis at around this time, and it is not difficult to see how such a clean-cut, sporty and stiff young man would take exception to the outrageous behaviour of the young John Betjeman. (Courtesy of Alpha Historica/Alamy Stock Photo)

This sheet of paper with drawings in blue ink by John Betjeman describes the three grades of churchmanship characterised by altar, times of worship, headgear and physiognomy, affiliation, vestments and stole. On the reverse is a note by John Betjeman: 'To laugh is light, not to laugh is deep. Light is bad, deep is good. That is what I learned, by implication, from my tutor. One was allowed to laugh at what he thought was bad. That is the privilege of an educated person. Light literature meant literature that was easy to read and ... meant you to laugh.'

This is a dig at his tutor C. S. Lewis, who regarded John Betjeman as frivolous and lacking in application, and who failed to support him when he failed the compulsory Divinity examination. This manuscript sheet, which gives an interesting insight into John Betjeman's attitudes and interests, is in a copy of *Lawn Sleeves: A Short Life of Samuel Wilberforce* by J. C. Hardwick (1933), which is inscribed to 'The Reverend Major, in remembrance of his two and a half years in the Ministry of the Church of England Reformed, from John Betjeman 1939.'

Right: Walters in the Turl, Oxford. This gentlemen's outfitters has been an Oxford institution for over 150 years and was a favourite place for John Betjeman to buy his silk ties.

Below: The High Street, Oxford. 'The High', as it is known, is the main thoroughfare in Oxford, curving elegantly from Magdalen Bridge up to Carfax. From the eighteenth-century bridge over the River Cherwell, you pass Magdalen College on the right, the Examination Schools and University College on the left, then Queens College, All Souls, the Church of St Mary the Virgin with its soaring thirteenth-century spire, Oriel College, numerous medieval buildings housing shops and offices, and the Mitre, a coaching inn built around 1600 over a thirteenth-century vault. It is one of the world's great streets. (Drawing by W. G. Blackall from *The Charm of Oxford* by J. Wells, London, 1920)

and concluded: 'I don't see how anyone with visual sensibility can live in Magdalen and be unmoved by architecture if their job is partly that of teaching an appreciation of English literature.' (Quoted in *Betjeman* by A. N. Wilson.) He painted his own eccentric portrait of Oxford and settled old scores in his guidebook, *An Oxford University Chest* (1938), which described the three Oxfords – 'Christminster', the old city; 'Motopolis', or the Cowley suburbs; and the university itself – and included chapters on undergraduates, dons and scouts as well as a gazetteer at the end. The book was illustrated by Osbert Lancaster's caricatures, line drawings and old prints and, above all, the evocative photographs of Lazlo Moholy-Nagy, a Hungarian-born member of the Bauhaus. It is typically Betjemanesque in

The High Street today reveals the same elegant curve and fine buildings as in 1920, but cars, vans and buses ruin the view. John Betjeman didn't like the motor car and thought it an intrusion in Oxford.

The view from the Broad Walk in Christchurch Meadows, with the spire of Christ Church Cathedral, the tower of Merton College Chapel and the Cathedral Choir School playing fields in the foreground. This is the beautiful environment that so captivated the young John Betjeman.

St Mary the Virgin from Oriel Square, Oxford, from a late nineteenth-century photograph.

Magdalen Bridge with moored punts sitting in the autumn sunshine after a busy summer.

its outlook and scope, and influenced later portrayals of Oxford, notably Dacre Balsdon's *Oxford Life* (1957) and James Morris's *Oxford* (1965).

But the person against whom Betjeman entertained the strongest negative feelings was Professor Nikolaus Pevsner, the German émigré and architectural writer who came to England in 1933 and quickly established himself as a formidable authority and academic art historian, publishing his *Pioneers of the Modern Movement from William Morris to Walter Gropius* in 1936, his *Outline of European Architecture* in 1942, and laying plans for his *Buildings of England* series, the first of which, *Cornwall, Nottinghamshire* and *Middlesex*, appeared in 1951.

Professor Sir Nikolaus Pevsner (1902–83) was a German Jewish refugee who moved to England in 1933 and became an academic historian of art and architecture, publishing many influential books and working on the monumental *Buildings of England* series for Penguin from 1945 onwards. With John Betjeman he was one of the founder members of the Victorian Society. (Courtesy of Wikimedia Commons)

Betjeman distrusted Pevsner for a number of reasons, mostly reprehensible, but his most honourable and cogent reason was that he felt that the Pevsner *Buildings of England* books missed the point. In Pevsner's ambition to categorise, analyse and comprehensively list all the significant buildings in the country, Betjeman felt that his treasured English landscape with all its beauty, idiosyncrasy, ancient, unregarded buildings and, above all, its people was being reduced to a vast and arid collection of museum exhibits. In his book *First and Last Loves* (John Murray, 1952) he complains, 'The Herr Professor – Doktors [i.e. Pevsner] are writing everything down for us, sometimes throwing in a little hurried pontificating too, so we need never bother to feel or think or see again.' And in chapter seven, 'Antiquarian Prejudice', he castigates what he calls 'the experts' as 'short-sighted, with the gift of turning life to death, interest to ashes'. I will refer briefly in chapter three to the long, drawn-out vendetta that Betjeman waged against Pevsner. It has been fully explored in Timothy Mowl's book *Stylistic Cold Wars* (John Murray, 2000) and in Susan Harries's splendid biography *Nikolaus Pevsner* (Chatto & Windus, 2011). Instead, I want to use this conflict of views to highlight the positive aspects of Betjeman's approach to the built environment, which I believe are in danger of being forgotten. Recent history has shown that Pevsner has decisively won the battle of the books, in that *The Buildings of England* series, since extended to cover Scotland, Ireland and Wales, is still very much in print, in a continual process of revision, and much admired across the world. By contrast, the *Shell Guides* started by Betjeman in collaboration with Jack Beddington, the Director of Publicity for Shell, and launched with the publication of *Cornwall* in 1934, are now all out of print and only available on the second-hand market. This is a sad irony considering that in their first five years, from 1934 to 1939, thirteen guides were published with innovative layout, photography and letterpress, which established Betjeman's reputation as a writer and topographer much more than his poetry did at the time.

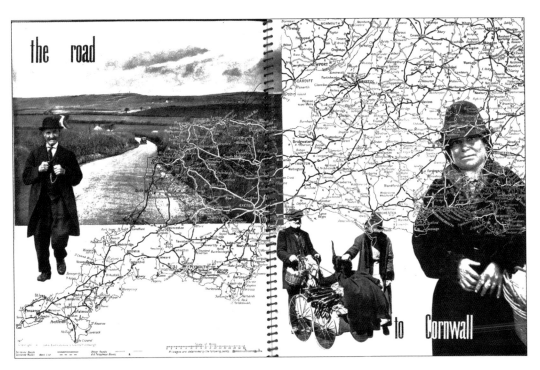

The Shell Guide to Cornwall (1934). The inside spread of John Betjeman's first guide is a montage of a map of the county with local figures to add 'colour' and modern lettering. He wanted the guides to be unstuffy, full of pictures and to include neglected eighteenth- and nineteenth-century buildings.

However, although Betjeman lost the battle of the guidebooks, it is my contention that with the passage of time he has won the war, in that cultural taste has changed and developed over the years since his death, so that we now value the intuitive and emotional response just as much if not more than the rational and the analytical.

As an example of this shift of approach, let me refer briefly to my own discipline of biblical studies. In the post-Enlightenment world, there was a strong emphasis on reason and scientific enquiry, which in the field of biblical interpretation led from the eighteenth century onwards to the rise of the historical-critical method of studying the scriptures. For much of the twentieth century, and certainly when I was studying theology at Oxford in the early 1970s, this narrowly academic approach to the text was dominant, but towards the end of the century, influenced by the rise of postmodernism (a collection of responses to the rationalism of modernism), there was a greater willingness to study the ancient texts in different and wider ways. We have seen the rise of, among other approaches, feminist interpretation, liberation theology, post-colonial analysis and reception history. The emphasis has moved from the text in context to the reader in context, and a realisation that we come to the Bible shaped by the world in which we live, the experiences we have had, the knowledge we have accumulated and the prejudices we have acquired.

This has also led to a renewed interest in the way medieval thinkers viewed scripture. When they read scripture, they would interrogate the text and ask themselves questions

19

such as: 'What is the inner meaning of this text for us now?' or 'What is God asking me to change in my life in response to this text?' This approach draws on the Platonic way of 'seeing', which involves active participation rather than detached observation. For instance, a predominantly preliterate age saw no reason to 'observe' a great medieval building such as Salisbury Cathedral from a safe distance. They built houses close up to the main entrance and looked at the building as participants, being prepared to become part of the drama it represented and being moved and challenged by what they were experiencing in front of them.

This more intuitive and subjective approach to scripture, and indeed literature generally, has an obvious parallel in the way we look at and study buildings. It was an approach that John Betjeman instinctively embraced, and in the field of architectural appreciation it is a tradition of emotional and subjective response that others have followed, notably Ian Nairn, Jonathan Meades and Gavin Stamp.

Jonathan Meades in his book *Museum Without Walls* describes Ian Nairn's approach as 'redbrick, tap-room aestheticism'. Nairn was a journalist, a self-taught commentator on architecture, who brought a poet's sensibility to his writing as well as an obstreperous and anarchic attitude to the established and the fashionable in architecture. In his wonderful guidebook *Nairn's London* (1966), he gives us a tour of London buildings based on his own partisan, visual and emotional response to what he sees around him. Nairn also wrote most of the *Buildings of England* volume on Surrey and collaborated with Nikolaus Pevsner on the West Sussex section of the original *Buildings of England* volume on Sussex, which again reveals his very personal, evocative and poetic response to this part of the county. Significantly however, he found himself increasingly out of sympathy with the Pevsner 'cataloguey' tradition and the need for ever more detailed descriptions, and withdrew from any further involvement with the series.

In a similar tradition Jonathan Meades (b. 1947) brings a journalistic, astringent and literary eye to his writing, driven by what he calls an 'incurable topophilia', a passionate and curious love of the world around him that believes 'there is no such thing as a boring place'.

Jonathan Meades wrote a fascinating essay on John Betjeman's influence on our perception of architecture and landscape in *Country Life* to celebrate the 100th anniversary of Betjeman's birth, in which he says:

> Just as he tirelessly opened our eyes to neglected architectural idioms so did he persuasively broaden our appetite for places. Places rather than mere architecture were his greatest forte: architecture, a component of places, was too limiting. Betjeman was excited by the humble, by the everyday, by the allegedly meretricious, by preposterous kitch, by fortuitous juxtapositions, by collisions of the bathetic and the sumptuous. He brought an aesthete's sensibility to bear on found objects which better behaved or less professionally opportunistic aesthetes would shy away from...

Gavin Stamp admired both Betjeman and Nairn, claiming that it was Betjeman who first inspired him to look at buildings when he was a schoolboy at Dulwich College. Stamp became a writer and architectural campaigner and took over the 'Piloti' column in *Private Eye* from Betjeman. Of those I have mentioned it is perhaps Stamp who most effectively took on Betjeman's mantle. Through his campaigning, writing and television work until his untimely death in 2017 he ensured that a concern for the quality of the built environment remained firmly on the public agenda.

All these writers share, to a degree, Betjeman's particular way of looking at buildings and places. While Gavin Stamp became Professor of Architecture at Glasgow University, he retained a strong sensibility to place and architectural worth. He, like John Betjeman, Ian Nairn and Jonathan Meades, liked passing subjective judgements – often acerbic, always acute – and he didn't much care whether they accorded with the established art-historical and aesthetic canon of the day. As Jonathan Meades has remarked, Betjeman's anti-intellectualism was itself a carefully chosen intellectual posture, combining a music hall persona with an encyclopaedic knowledge of the obscure and forgotten artists, writers and architects of the eighteenth and nineteenth centuries who informed so much of his own outlook and writing.

Above all, as I mentioned earlier, Betjeman's response to buildings and landscape was mystical and poetic. I think that this is what Harry Williams was alluding to in the dedication of his book *Becoming What I Am* to John Betjeman, 'who likes dim things'. Betjeman often used the adjective 'dim' and always as a compliment. The word 'dim' can encompass what is obscure, and Betjeman certainly liked obscure writers, like the Manx poet Thomas Edward Brown, and obscure buildings such as neglected Methodist chapels, Georgian terraces and unknown Victorian architects.

'Dim' can also reference the dark or forgotten corners and details of buildings and places that Betjeman loved to notice. It suggests too the 'dim religious light' of Christian faith. Early on in his life, through meeting the rector of St Ervan's Church, the Revd Wilfred Johnson, while on family holidays in Cornwall, Betjeman was opened up to the power of Celtic mysticism, the holy places of Cornwall and the enticing aesthetic-cum-religious experience of Anglo-Catholicism.

This sense of the mystical, in which 'past and present were enwrapped in one', can be found in the early *Shell Guides*, especially those for Cornwall and Devon. *The Shell Guide to Cornwall* has a section on 'The Age of Saints' and in *Devon* there is folklore, superstitious fun and pixies, while in the later *Wiltshire* guide Edith Oliver makes a number of references to ghosts in the gazetteer.

The importance of the supernatural, and a belief in 'thin places' where the spiritual breaks through into the temporal run like a thread through Betjeman's best creative work, his TV series *ABC of Churches* (1960–68), his *Collins Guide to English Parish Churches* (1958), his lifelong poetic output, and his later TV documentary *A Passion for Churches* (1974). It is impossible to fully understand and appreciate Betjeman without taking account of the importance of the life of faith to him. This committed, holistic, spiritual approach to the world around him and his delight in out of the way detail comes through most vividly in his television work. For the first programme in the *ABC of Churches* series, transmitted on 15 May 1960, Betjeman visits St Michael's Aldbourne in Wiltshire. He takes us on a journey through time as he wanders around the building. 'Gradually I begin to learn the history of the place ... I can picture what England was like then ... Looking at Aldbourne Church is like a detective story...' He points out the tomb of John Stone in the chancel, the vicar of the parish who died in 1510 and left to the parish 'a new chalice that I bought late in London', and Betjeman shows us the chalice, still in use. He asks us to imagine the church as it might have been at the time of the Reformation, he points out the eighteenth-century

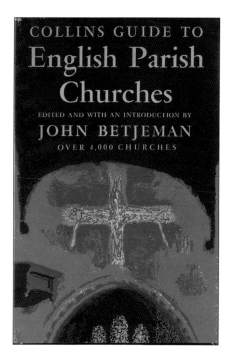

Cover of the *Collins Guide to English Parish Churches* (1958). John Betjeman and John Piper were keen to produce a handy guide to a selection from the 16,000 parish churches in England, judged on their atmosphere and aesthetic merit. The 'spirit' of the book, according to John Betjeman, was to list churches that had escaped 'restoration' by the Victorians, but also to notice Georgian and Victorian buildings. His friend Osbert Lancaster had given him a watercolour of an unrestored church, which he wanted to form the basis of the cover. In the end a detail from a painting by John Piper was used, with the whole wrapper designed by Clifford and Rosemary Ellis. John Betjeman collected material for the book over a number of years and enlisted a number of contributors to write up individual counties.

fire engine, and ends by calling our attention to the bells, which for centuries have called across the Wiltshire Downs. 'Listen to them...'

Betjeman was a consummate performer who wanted you to share what really mattered to him. His style was conversational and fun, and he knew the value of suspense and the power of silence. He had the journalist's skill of summing things up in pithy and memorable sentences. Above all he wanted people to look again at the buildings and the environment that they so often took for granted and failed to value. Within the scope of this book it is difficult to fully evoke his character and personality, but in what follows I shall attempt to build a picture of how John Betjeman looked at the world around him and how he tried to share his scholarly knowledge of architecture and topography in a way that conveyed pleasure even to those who don't read books on architecture. I shall look at some of the places that were important to him and reflect on how these places formed his outlook and shaped his architectural vision. Along the way I shall be briefly autobiographical because so many of the places that were important to John Betjeman are places that played an important part in my own life and helped to form my own tastes and outlook.

As his biographer Bevis Hillier has noticed, Betjeman had the same idea about architectural appreciation as Sigmund Freud had about the human psyche: that experiences in early childhood are crucially formative. 'What makes you like architecture are the things you have seen and reacted to as a child.'

So we begin with childhood memories, formative experiences and influences, and especially with north Cornwall, scene of childhood holidays, 'Cornish air, Soft Cornish rains, and silence after steam ... Safe Cornish holidays before the storm!' (*Summoned by Bells*, chapter four).

1

Childhood and Cornwall

Some of the happiest memories of my own childhood relate to family holidays. In summer during the 1950s my parents took my brother and me down to Salcombe, in South Devon, then a small fishing village close to the mouth of the Kingsbridge Estuary. The journey began when we were collected from our home in Pinner, Middlesex, by Mr Allen in his stylish Riley, the seats smelling of well-worn leather, our suitcases safely stowed in the boot. He drove us up to Paddington station in central London where we boarded a steam-hauled express to the West Country, which we left at Brent Junction to catch the branch line train to Kingsbridge. This single-track branch line opened in 1893 and closed amid much local opposition in 1963. It followed the scenic route of the River Avon, with delightful little stations at Avonwick, Gara Bridge and Loddiswell. At Kingsbridge station another car would meet us and drive us to Salcombe to the guest house run by Mrs Spiers. Then began two weeks of seaside delight, exploring the coves and beaches of the area, crossing to East Portlemouth in the clinker-built ferry boat run by Victor the ferryman and walking to Mill Bay, or trekking to the Gara Rock Hotel for High Tea, or visiting the little sweet and toy shop in Salcombe High Street. I have a vivid memory of waking up one year on the first morning of our holiday and, in my half-awake state, thinking that I would have to get up and prepare for school, only to realise with a delicious spasm of recognition that I was in Salcombe and that we were on holiday! I think John Betjeman would have clearly recognised the joy and exhilaration of that moment.

As well as our annual summer holiday my parents usually took us away for a few days over the Easter holidays, often visiting the Cotswolds or travelling around Kent. Whether staying at Burford in Oxfordshire or Chilham in Kent, we explored the many churches in these areas, and my young eyes were opened to the delight of villages like Eastleach Martin and Eastleach Turville – two picturesque hamlets divided by the River Leach and crossed by a medieval footbridge. Both little churches are full of atmosphere. It was on such holidays, and picnic outings into the Chiltern Hills during the school holidays that my passion for churches was kindled, which was further encouraged and fed by John Betjeman's *Collins Guide to English Parish Churches* (1958) and his TV series *An ABC of Churches*, which began in 1960. I still remember watching one of the nine-part *ABC of Churches* series, which began with a shot of Betjeman walking up the path to

Eastleach Turville, Gloucestershire. A drawing, possibly by John Betjeman, in one of John Piper's notebooks, showing the churchyard path and lamp bracket. The two hamlets of Eastleach Martin and Eastleach Turville are set on either side of a clear stream and connected by a flat stone bridge known as Keble's Bridge, in honour of the Tractarian writer and poet who was a curate here. An idyllic setting. (Courtesy of Tate Gallery Archive)

the church porch, commenting briefly on the exterior of the building, and then turning directly to the camera, beckoning conspiratorially and saying, 'Now, come inside...' I was entranced, feeling that John Betjeman wanted me personally to share his knowledge and enthusiasm, and as eager to experience the excitement of the interior as he was. That sense of anticipation when visiting a church has never left me.

*****

John Betjeman was born on 28 August 1906 at No. 52 Parliament Hill Mansions, Hampstead. His mother Bess was the daughter of an artificial flower manufacturer from Highbury, and his father Ernest Betjeman ran the family firm G. Betjemann & Sons, cabinetmakers and silversmiths based on Pentonville Road. His family being firmly 'in trade', John Betjeman was part of a middle-class Edwardian world in which his parents undoubtedly wished to rise up the social scale, but expected him as the only son to carry on the family business. Aged three, he moved to No. 31 West Hill, Highgate, and in spite of the constraints of family life, the beatings meted out by his nurse Maud and the bullying of fellow schoolboys, Betjeman retained very happy memories of his home on leafy West Hill.

As an only child, Betjeman suffered from loneliness and felt isolated from other people, including his parents. He sought refuge in 'inanimate things', especially his teddy bear Archibald, in cultivating his imagination, and in reading and writing. He began reading poetry, devouring Keats, Longfellow, William Cowper and Wordsworth, and embarked upon writing his own poetry.

Then in 1917, aged eleven, he was sent to the Dragon Preparatory School in Oxford, where he boarded for three years. This happened because his parents had come to know the headmaster H. E. Lynam through holidaying at Trebetherick in north Cornwall, where they both had holiday homes. The Dragon was a much more congenial environment for Betjeman once he had got over his initial homesickness. He was taken under H. E. Lynam's wing, who encouraged his interest in literature. He was also given the freedom to explore the architecture of the city of Oxford and the surrounding villages. With his friend Ronald Wright he bicycled off to churches in Oxford and was soon au fait with the names of architectural terms, such as Norman, Early English, Decorated, Perpendicular and all the varied fixtures and fittings of an ancient church. This interest was encouraged and tutored by his housemaster Gerald Haynes, who took him on bicycle excursions to village churches around Oxfordshire. Haynes had a particular liking for Norman architecture and took photographs on his big plate camera, which he later used as illustrations for his lectures to the boys. Above all, Haynes was a natural teacher with a 'power to share joys of his own, churches and botany, with those of us whose tastes he could inform'. Betjeman felt he owed his love of architecture to Gerald Haynes and dedicated his book *First and Last Loves* in 1952 to his memory.

During his time at the Dragon Betjeman's parents moved to Chelsea, rising another rung up the social ladder, and while Betjeman missed Highgate, the move meant that he now lived close to his friend Ronald Wright. Together they explored London, visiting its many churches and travelling all over the London Underground railway system, even to its furthest extremities in Buckinghamshire and Essex and Middlesex. During school holidays Betjeman would find his way to deserted City of London churches for evensong and browse the second-hand bookshops on the Essex and Farringdon roads, pursuing his book-collecting hobby. In this he was encouraged by his father who once gave him *The Churches of London* by George Godwin, inscribed: 'To my dear boy in the hope that his appreciation of all that is beautiful will never fade.' (Quoted in Bevis Hillier's *Young Betjeman*, 1988, p. 49.) These early book browsing expeditions gave Betjeman a lifelong love of book collecting, and over the years he gathered an impressive library of books and folios on architecture and topography.

Every summer the Betjemans went on holiday to Cornwall by the London & South Western Railway, travelling from Waterloo to Wadebridge. There they descended from the London train and were taken by a horse brake to their holiday house at Trebetherick. At first they stayed in a boarding house, but in 1929 Ernest Betjeman built a house, in the Arts and Crafts style, 'Undertown', on land near Daymer Bay. John Betjeman enjoyed the usual seaside pursuits of building sandcastles, exploring rock pools and playing games with other children on holiday. As he grew a little older he would bicycle off to look at the flora and fauna of north Cornwall and learn their exotic vocabulary of names, many of which reappear in his poetry. Nature gradually gave way to church architecture as he grew towards adolescence, stimulated by his visit to St Enodoc, the church near his holiday home, built in 1430 on the site of the saint's cell, and then slowly buried over the succeeding centuries in the encroaching sand. In the nineteenth century, in order to ensure that it remained legally open for worship a clergyman was lowered through a hole in the roof to hold a service once a year. The small slate spire peeps over the links and sandy beach of Daymer Bay. Inside it has been much restored by J. P. St Aubyn, but there is a cut-down medieval screen and a Norman font. Betjeman bicycled far and wide 'on sunny antiquarian afternoons' to visit churches in north Cornwall, including the delights

The former station buildings at Wadebridge, Cornwall. Every summer the Betjeman family arrived at Wadebridge station by the London & South Western train from Waterloo. As the train arrived at the station he would look out of the carriage window to see the fifteenth-century bridge over the River Camel. The present buildings date from 1895. The line was closed to passenger traffic in 1967 and the station building is now used as a day centre and contains many bits of Betjeman memorabilia in the entrance lobby. (Courtesy of Stuart Vallis)

A view of the medieval arched bridge at Wadebridge at night. It was built around 1485 and is 320 feet long on seventeen arches. The foundations are said to have been sunk on packs of wool. (Courtesy of Stuart Vallis)

Above: John Betjeman in Cornwall. (Courtesy of Jonathan Stedall)

Right: Daymer Bay, Trebetherick, Cornwall. This was where the young John Betjeman played as a child with his other holiday friends, building sandcastles, climbing the cliffs and playing in the rock pools. It remained a very important place for him all his life, retaining happy memories and a sense of security. (Courtesy of Stuart Vallis)

One of John Betjeman's favourite churches, St Enodoc at Trebetherick, nestles among the sand dunes in the middle of the golf course. It was built in the twelfth century, with later additions, on the site of the saint's cell and can only be approached on foot across the links. An architecturally unremarkable church, it nevertheless features in a number of John Betjeman's poems and prose writings, and is where his parents and the poet himself are buried. His grave is marked by a Delabole slate headstone carved by Simon Verity. (Courtesy of Stuart Vallis)

St Protus and St Hyacinth, Blisland. Inland, along wooded lanes you come upon the village of Blisland, with Georgian cottages around an elm-shaded green. On the southern side the church looks over the valley, with its fifteenth-century tower and a churchyard full of gravestones. (Courtesy of Stuart Vallis)

of St Protus and St Hyacinth, Blisland, a church that always retained a special place in his heart. 'I was a boy when I first saw it. I shall never forget that first visit – bicycling to the inland and unvisited parts of Cornwall from my home by the sea.'

Betjeman wrote about it lyrically in his *Shell Guide to Cornwall*:

> Streams from the moor descend in steep wooded valleys westward and high hedged lanes with hazel and honeysuckle and ferny sides leave the moor for the valleys whose waters flow into the Camel. On the slope of one of these valleys is the village of granite cottages, mostly Georgian and earlier, round a big goose-green planted with tall thin elms and ash. Below its southern slope is the church with fifteenth century tower – a snug rectory is west of it.

However, it isn't just its setting but the interior that exerts a powerful effect. The effect of the church as you enter it is dazzling. There is a delightful mixture of styles, from Norman to the twentieth century, granite pillars leaning this way and that, a richly carved barrel roof, and across the whole width of the church a highly painted wooden screen with rood loft above, looking authentically medieval but in fact a sensitive reconstruction

Above left: St Protus and St Hyacinth, Blisland. Inside the church the effect is one of colour and mystery. The pulpit and screen and loft that extends across the whole church is by the twentieth-century architect F. C. Eden, with the main altar in the Italian Renaissance style by John Ninian Comper. It feels like a genuine late medieval church in Cornwall, with Renaissance features, and as a convincing restoration could hardly be bettered. John Betjeman enthused about the church in his Shell and Collins guides. (Courtesy of Stuart Vallis)

Above right: St Protus and St Hyacinth, Blisland. A peaceful view of the south-west corner of the church, showing the Norman circular font and handsome window. (Courtesy of Stuart Vallis)

by F. C. Eden between 1896 and 1930. Betjeman felt that Eden had a vision of the church as it would have been in medieval times. 'It is a living church whose beauty makes you gasp, whose silence brings you to your knees, even if you kneel on the hard stone and slate of the floor, worn smooth by generations of worshippers.'

Although Betjeman loved St Enodoc and St Protus and St Hyacinth, Blisland, perhaps his favourite church was St Endellion, near to Trebetherick: 'A windswept parish high on the Atlantic coast.' 'St Endellion! St Endellion! The name is like a ring of bells.' So began a BBC broadcast by Betjeman in 1949. It was the music of the ring of six bells that enticed his ears as he arrived in Cornwall by car. 'It was,' he said, 'a welcome to Cornwall and in front of us the sun was setting over Gulland and making the Atlantic at Polzeath and Pentire glow like a copper shield.' And he quotes approvingly, both in his broadcast

Granite signpost announcing the parish of Blisland. (Courtesy of Stuart Vallis)

St Endellion, Cornwall. The church whose bells John Betjeman felt welcomed him to Cornwall stands high up on the windswept coastline surrounded by a churchyard full of Georgian headstones. Inside the nave is low and wide with a wagon roof, slate floors and clear glass in the windows. In this view the Endelienta Ensemble are practising for a concert and playing Mozart's *Symphony No. 1*. A church where the arts are celebrated and which, as John Betjeman remarked, seems to 'go on praying day and night whether there are people in it or not'. (Courtesy of Stuart Vallis)

and in his *Shell Guide*, a rhyme painted on a board in the ringing chamber, written in Georgian times:

Let's all in love and friendship hither come,
Whilst the shrill treble calls to thundering Tom,

St Endellion, Cornwall. A popular means of personal commemoration in Cornwall was to place a holy water stoup bearing the donor's arms next to the main door of the church, to encourage those entering to remember the donor. By the south door at St Endellion is this delightful stoup carved in dark blue Catacleuse stone, with the coats of arms of Roscarrock and related families, the Chenduits and Trevenors, decorated with acorn motifs. (Courtesy of Stuart Vallis)

> And since bells are for modest recreation,
> Let's rise and ring and fall to admiration.

Inside the church, 'old roofs remain, the windows have clear glass, the floors are slate, old bench ends are in the nave, and good solid new ones in the aisles'. In the south aisle is what is supposed to be the shrine of St Endelienta, the Celtic virgin saint to whom the church is dedicated and about whom an Elizabethan writer composed a touching hymn. Around the church in the churchyard there is a forest of upright Delabole slate headstones, lettered in beautiful flowing script, and nearby are the rectory and prebendal cottages, indicating that it used to be a collegiate church served by a college of priests, the prebends of Marny, Trehaverock, Endellion and Bodmin. It is a particularly satisfying cluster of buildings, with just that sense of aesthetic appeal and mystery that Betjeman found so powerful. In his BBC broadcast he asks, 'Why does St Endellion seem to go on praying when there is no-one in it? The Blessed Sacrament is not reserved here, yet the building is alive.' And, he adds, 'Sancta Endelienta, *ora pro nobis!*'

North Cornwall, with 'its little valleys where there are old churches and the wells of Celtic saints who lived 1400 years ago,' a land 'soaked in Christianity,' the land of Parson Robert Stephen Hawker of Morwenstow and Revd Sabine Baring-Gould, both embodiments of a mixture of Celtic and Anglo-Catholic Christianity, exercised a strong influence on the young Betjeman, nurtured his love of church architecture and fed his mystic longings.

St Nonna, Altarnun, Cornwall. The church with its lofty tower is set in the valley of the Penpont Water and reached by an old humpbacked bridge. The village is large and has old stone cottages and a Methodist chapel (now converted to a private house) with a portrait bust of John Wesley over the door. (Courtesy of Stuart Vallis)

In 1948 Betjeman wrote:

> Some learn their faith from books, some from relations, some (a very few) learn it at school. I learned mine from church crawling. Indeed it was through looking at churches that I came to believe in the reason why churches were built, and why, despite neglect and contempt, innovation and business bishops, they still survive...

He wrote this as part of a broadcast about St Protus and St Hyacinth, Blisland, and in his introductory remarks he added his suggestions for how to go about church crawling. First of all, you must have the right instruments, especially a 1-inch Ordnance Survey map, because it will tell you whether the church has a tower or a spire, and, if it is tucked away at the end of a lane, how to get to it.

In another article, entitled 'Church Crawling', Betjeman adds to the list of essential instruments for the church crawler:

> 1) a notebook in which you can sketch and write remarks; 2) field glasses for viewing roofs and stained glass... and an unprejudiced eye.
>
> The next thing you need is an eye. Please notice that. An eye. Not knowledge of styles of architecture, of squinches, squints, piscinae, aumbries and all the other jargon of the church guidebooks. Look at the church for what it is: a place of worship and a piece of architecture combined ... Instead of bothering about dates and what the guidebooks say is old, use your own eyes.

St Nonna, Altarnun, Cornwall. The church possesses a large collection of early sixteenth-century bench ends, showing instruments of the Passion, St Michael, local figures including a piper playing, a fiddler and angels holding shields. They were all carved by Robert Daye around 1530, a known local artist. (Courtesy of Stuart Vallis)

In another 1949 article Betjeman had written: 'There are three ways of looking at a church–as a place of worship, as a historical record, as architecture.' He conjures up the fictional church of Bagby St Petroc and gradually takes us back in time, first to 150 years ago with whitewashed walls, clear glass in the windows, a band in the west gallery and the rector declaiming from the three-decker pulpit; then back again three centuries earlier to medieval times, with no pews, the priest at the altar behind the rood screen, and side altars belonging to the town guilds; then back to the twelfth-century, thick-walled Norman church; and finally back to the original wooden Saxon structure, built on a pagan burial ground. Running through this fictional history is the sense of the continuity of worship within the successive buildings. This highlights the conviction Betjeman held that he liked the look of a church best of all when it was being used: 'Human figures giving scale and purpose to the glorious decoration designed for the service of God.'

What we might call Betjeman's 'sacramental politics' is based on a particular Anglican quality of embracing mystery, ambiguity and a refusal to simplify, while holding to a strongly sacramental approach to theology and worship. A sacrament is an outward and visible sign of an inward and spiritual grace, based on the belief that, in Harry Williams' words, 'ordinary things are not ordinary at all', but point to the mystery at the heart of human existence. Betjeman had expressed this conviction very directly in an article in *The Studio* in February 1937 when he stated that architecture is 'the outward and visible form of inward and spiritual grace or disgrace'. This sense of spiritual mystery harmonised between faith and nature was something that Betjeman found in Cornwall – its churches, coastline and countryside – as a boy and which he subsequently found echoed and

BODMIN CHURCH AND ST. THOMAS'S CHAPEL

St Petroc, Bodmin, Cornwall. John Betjeman loved Cornish saints, and St Petroc was among the most important. In the sixth century AD he came over from Ireland and landed at Padstow, but after a dream on a pilgrimage to Rome and Jerusalem he returned to Cornwall and settled at Bodmin by a holy well and converted the king, Constantine, whom he met when the king was out hunting. Petroc founded a monastery at Bodmin, but the present church mostly dates from the fifteenth century. Inside is the tomb of Prior Vyvyan (d. 1533), the last but one Prior of Bodmin, of black Catacleuse stone and grey marble.

John Betjeman loved the unusual, and here in St Mabyn are the ancient churchwardens' chest, the village stocks and the wedding broom for the ceremony of 'Jumping the Broom', in which bride and groom signify their entry into their new life by sweeping away their former concerns and stepping over the broom into a new adventure together. (Courtesy of Stuart Vallis)

re-echoed in the churches, villages and cities of England as he visited them over the course of his lifetime.

In many of his poems, articles and radio broadcasts this sacramental sense comes through. In poems such as 'St Saviour's, Aberdeen Park, Highbury, London N', 'A Lincolnshire Church' and 'Sunday Morning, King's Cambridge' the poet moves from description to adoration, from observer to worshipper. In *A Lincolnshire Church* (1958) the speaker stands on the church threshold, opens the door and finds a spiritual presence focused in the Reserved Sacrament. 'There where the white light flickers, Our Creator is with us yet.'

This, to Betjeman's objective – presence – transforms what is in reality not a very exciting building, architecturally speaking, into a place of profound significance, transfigured by the worship going on inside it. It is instructive to compare these poems by Betjeman with the major poem 'Church Going' written by his contemporary Philip Larkin.

Philip Larkin (1922–85) was the senior librarian at the Brynmor Jones Library at the University of Hull, and himself a distinguished poet. He was a very English writer with a strongly pessimistic streak, influenced by Thomas Hardy, W. B. Yeats and W. H. Auden. He admired John Betjeman's poetry, and the feeling was mutual. In June 1964 Betjeman took part in a BBC *Monitor* programme about Philip Larkin, and the two men shared thoughts about poetry, death and churches. Larkin confessed that he too had always been an inveterate church crawler, and Betjeman recited Larkin's poem 'Church Going', which appeared in his second collection of poems, *The Less Deceived*, published in 1955.

In this lyric poem the speaker visits old churches out of curiosity rather than devotion. He still retains an 'awkward reverence' but doesn't understand the arcane details of the architecture, fixtures and fittings. He feels a sense of sadness both because these buildings are gradually falling into disuse and because of the ignorance of ordinary people about their own inheritance of faith.

In spite of this sense of loss the speaker ends with a moving affirmation of the enduring importance of these buildings:

> A serious house on serious earth it is,
> In whose blent air all our compulsions meet,
> Are recognised and robed as destinies.
> And that much never can be obsolete,
> Since someone will forever be surprising,
> A hunger in himself to be more serious.

Stephen Gardner has remarked that 'the defining aspect of post-war Britain in this monumental poem is the loss of a cohesive cultural identity once sustained by a common faith'. In spite of the poet's agnostic cynicism, he recognises that churches are places where we can satisfy our hunger to be serious, where the crisis points of life – birth, marriage and death – can be marked with dignity and ritual, and where we can encounter holy mystery, although he remains ambivalent about his own feelings.

Betjeman, while quoting Larkin's words with approval, wanted to go much further. He was highly critical of English indifference to religion and became an effective apologist for the religious dimension to life in general, and the Christian faith in particular, as effective an apologist in his own way as C. S. Lewis, his other abiding bête noir.

Betjeman set out his personal creed in a number of places, perhaps most movingly in a BBC broadcast on the Home Service on Christmas Day 1947, in which he first set down thoughts that were eventually distilled into his memorable poem 'Christmas', published in 1954. In it he begins by reminiscing about past Christmases and then quite suddenly becomes very personal.

I cannot believe that I am surrounded by a purposeless accident. On a clear night I look up at the stars and, remembering amateur astronomy, know that the Milky Way is the rest of this universe and that the light from some of the stars has taken years to reach this planet. When I consider that the light from the sun twenty million miles away takes eight and a half minutes, the consequent immensity of this universe seems intolerable. And then on any day about now, I can turn over a piece of decaying wood in our garden and see myriapods, insects and bugs, startled out of sluggish winter torpor by my motion. Each is perfectly formed and adapted to its life. From the immensity of the stars to the perfection of an insect – I cannot believe that I am surrounded by a purposeless accident.

But can I believe this most fantastic story of all, that the Maker of the stars and of the centipedes, became a Baby in Bethlehem not so long ago? No time ago at all, when you reckon the age of the earth. Well it's asking a lot. If I weren't such a highbrow it would be easier. No man of intelligence can believe such a thing. A child of Jewish parents the Creator of the Universe? Absurd.

But if it is not true, why was I born? And if it is true, nothing else is of so much importance.

Beyond my reason, beyond my emotions, beyond my intellect I know that this peculiar story is true. Architecture brings it home to me. I suppose because architecture is, with poetry, my chief interest.

King's College, Cambridge. This magnificent chapel, built through the munificence of Henry VI, VII and VIII, always takes the breath away, and inspired one of John Betjeman's best poems. Might, majesty, grace and glory are celebrated in the soaring shafts of the fan vaulting, hung with crowns, the Tudor portcullis and crosses. As Norman Scarfe remarks in the *Shell Guide to Cambridgeshire*, the antechapel and chapel are divided by the screen, 'but united by a fantastic triumph of height and breadth, weightlessness and weight, in an inevitability of proportion that marks it among the finest buildings of the world.' To enter the chapel is to experience, in John Betjeman's memorable phrase, 'Eternity contained in Time and coloured glass.' (Courtesy of Stuart Vallis)

He illustrates this personal truth with an account of his visit to a Christmas carol service at King's College, Cambridge, 'The swansong of Perpendicular architecture', a vast, superbly proportioned, mysterious building. As the congregation stood waiting for the choir to enter, the first verse of 'Once in Royal David's City' was sung by a boy treble beyond the screen. 'It was clear, pure, distinct. And as I heard it, I knew once more – knew despite myself – that this story was the Truth.'

To Betjeman the powerful combination of architecture and living worship was what made churches such important and resonant places. In particular he admired the Church of England's role as the storehouse of English history and tradition, because it embodied the great narrative of English history, 'always truer in stone and glass than what you read in books'.

Interior of the chapel at King's College, Cambridge. The chapel soars to a height of 80 feet and is 40 feet wide, giving an impression of loftiness and weightlessness. John Wastell was the master mason, who for the final phase of construction created the great vault and the pinnacles on the buttresses. (Courtesy of Stuart Vallis)

2

London and the Railways

London

From the age of around twelve, in the 1960s, in the school holidays, my brother and I often took the Metropolitan Line train from our home in Pinner to Baker Street and explored London together, usually meeting our father for lunch near Smithfield Market, because his office was nearby. We enjoyed the freedom of walking around Fleet Street and Holborn, exploring the alleys and entrances that still echoed the old medieval street pattern, seeing the Old Cheshire Cheese tavern where Dr Johnson used to hold court and visiting his house tucked away in Bolt Court. We tramped the streets of Paddington and Marylebone, the narrow thoroughfares behind Regent Street just as Carnaby Street was becoming the trendy place to shop, and exploring the many hidden corners of the City of London with its fine churches, livery halls, Guildhall and Mansion House, the Monument to the Great Fire of London and narrow alleyways leading down to the River Thames. At this period the Port of London was still busy with shipping and signs of wartime bomb damage were evident – derelict churchyards and bomb sites turned into temporary car parks or left as wasteland where wild flowers grew in abundance. Off Thames Street alleys with names like Trig Lane, Stew Lane and Coffee House Alley led down to the surging waters of the Thames. Beyond the Wren church of St James Garlickhythe and further on St Magnus the Martyr (redolent of incense), there was Billingsgate Fish Market with its pungent smells. After a day exploring these exciting places my brother and I would eventually return to Smithfield to meet our father at the end of his working day. The City was a place of bustle, style, particular smells and sounds, and the mysterious sense of important activity taking place behind the elegant façades of city banks and livery halls. The many alleyways of the City invited further exploration: narrow openings that often led to little shops or taverns or small cafés, and every so often the tower or spire of a Wren church peeping out from the rooftops and completing the vista. In the 1950s and '60s the artist and writer Geoffrey Fletcher recorded the buildings, characters and sights of the City, the Thames and other hidden delights of London in articles written for *The Daily Telegraph*, *The Sphere* and other journals, which were then published in book form. His wonderfully evocative drawings inspired our juvenile wanderings and perfectly complemented the prose and poetry of John Betjeman.

Wine Office Court, Fleet Street, London. Dr Samuel Johnson said of London: 'If you wish to have a just notion of the magnitude of this great city you must not be satisfied with seeing its great streets and squares but must survey the innumerable little lanes and courts.' This court takes its name from the Excise Office, which was here until 1665. Nearby lived Dr Johnson and Oliver Goldsmith, and Johnson's friends often visited – Joshua Reynolds, Edward Gibbon David Garrick, James Boswell and others. The Cheshire Cheese public house still survives largely unchanged, a corner of old London that John Betjeman knew well. (Pen and ink drawing by Geoffrey Fletcher, 13 November 1968; © Estate of Geoffrey Fletcher)

The Old Wine Shades, Martin Lane, London. This is one of the oldest pubs in London, built in 1663 and a survivor of the Great Fire of 1666, complete with an underground tunnel connecting it with the River Thames. Geoffrey Fletcher's evocative drawing was made in March 1970 at a time when John Betjeman knew the pub. It was just the sort of characterful spot that gave him such pleasure in the City. (©Estate of Geoffrey Fletcher)

In his introduction to *The English Town in the Last Hundred Years* (CUP, 1956), John Betjeman wrote:

Looking at places is not for me just going to the church or the castle or the 'places of interest' mentioned in the guide book, but walking along the streets and lanes as well, just as in a country house I do not like to see state rooms only, but the passage to the billiard room, where the Spy cartoons are, and the bedrooms where I note the hairbrushes of the owner and the sort of hair-oil he uses. My hunt in a town is not just for one particular thing as an antiquary might look for Romanesque tympana, an art historian for a particular phase of baroque, or an architect for le Corbusier, but it is for the whole town ... I like to see the railway station, the town hall, the suburbs, the shops, the signs of local crafts being carried on in backyards. I like to be able to know for certain where to place what I am looking at.

Butterfield Rectory, Burleigh Street, Covent Garden, London. William Butterfield designed this parsonage for St Michael's, Burleigh Street, an ingenious plan on a very constricted site. Narrow and tall, built of red brick with yellow bands and stone dressings. Later converted as a London house for the Community of the Resurrection. John Betjeman championed Butterfield and other Victorian architects at a time when they were deeply unfashionable. (Pen and ink drawing by Geoffrey Fletcher, 27 September 1968; © Estate of Geoffrey Fletcher)

For Betjeman his fundamental interest was human life, the people who used, lived in and inhabited the buildings and places he so enjoyed visiting and describing. This was particularly true of London, the city in which he was born and grew up, which he explored with his boyhood friend Ronnie Wright and where he later established a bolthole in the Square Mile at No. 43 Cloth Fair in Smithfield. This became his London base for twenty years, and from here he explored the nooks and crannies of London, especially its churches. He said, 'Since I was a boy of twelve I have visited the City churches again and again, so that I can remember the interior of every one.'

In a *Spectator* article of 5 November 1954 Betjeman described the City churches as he knew them both before and after wartime damage. He described the surviving churches that evoked the atmosphere of the medieval city – St Bartholomew the Great and St Ethelburga's, Bishopsgate. He lamented the blackened Norman interior of St Bart's and the clutter of what he described as 'semi-sacred impedimenta', so familiar to those who love the Church of England. The interior of St Bart's the Great is now much improved and St Ethelburga's, badly damaged by an IRA bomb in 1993, has been gloriously restored and brought back to life in the last twenty years. Betjeman summed up what he was able to visit in 1954 as follows:

Wren rebuilt fifty churches after the [Great] fire [of London]. Before the Germans came we had ourselves destroyed nineteen of these. The Germans completely gutted seventeen more Wren churches, and there are now only fourteen with their roofs on, and of these three are still shut to the public, which leaves us with eleven Wren churches open to us in the City, and precious indeed they are.

Above left: Cloth Fair, Smithfield. When much of Cloth Fair was redeveloped most of the old houses disappeared, except for this old gabled corner house, saved by Lord Mottistone and Paul Paget in the 1930s. They bought the whole street, and Paget's father, when he retired as Bishop of Chester, moved into No. 39. John Betjeman came to lunch and was so taken with the area he moved into No. 43 in August 1954. Remnants of the earlier buildings remain in The Hand and Shears' pub and one or two small alleys leading into Smithfield. Across the road is the bulk of St Bartholemew the Great, one of the few medieval churches remaining in the City.

Above right: St Bartholomew's Hospital. The manuscript of John Betjeman's poem in praise of St Bart's, the hospital near his home in Cloth Fair where he became a regular ward visitor, a kind and generous gesture that was hidden from the rest of the world.

One day John Betjeman was waiting in the hospital to see one of the consultant surgeons, John Wickham (1927–2017), a pioneer of keyhole surgery. He suggested that John Betjeman should write a poem about Bart's while he waited, and this was the result:

> The ghost of Rahere still walks in Bart's
> It gives an impulse to generous hearts,
> It looks on pain with a pitying eye,
> It makes us never afraid to die.
>
> Eight hundred years of compassion and care
> Have hallowed its fountain, stones and square.
> Pray for us all as we near the Gate,
> St Bart the Less and St Bart the Great.

John Betjeman loved the two churches associated with the hospital and regularly attended St Bartholomew the Great. Rahere was court jester to Henry I, who founded the priory church in 1123. The poem celebrates the ghost of Rahere, which 'teaches us never to fear to die'. (Courtesy of Ann Wickham and Fr Marcus Walker, Rector of St Bartholomew the Great)

St Stephen's, Walbrook, City of London. Sir Christopher Wren designed the dome of St Stephen's before he tackled St Paul's Cathedral. The plain rectangle of the interior is broken up by sixteen columns, giving interesting vistas and creating separate nave, sanctuary, aisles and central space. The pulpit, altar rails and font are all contemporary with the church. Full of elegance and light, it was one of John Betjeman's favourite City churches.

Thankfully, a number of fire-bombed churches, including St Bride's and St Mary-le-Bow, were restored after the war, but still Betjeman's favourites were St Mary-at-Hill, St Magnus the Martyr, St Margaret Lothbury and St Stephen Walbrook. Sadly, the almost untouched interior of St Mary-at-Hill, with its box pews, sword rests, west gallery and fine pulpit and sounding board, was gutted by fire in the 1980s and, although restored, is bereft of those handsome fittings that gave the interior such character and charm.

Betjeman's memory stretched back to the years just after the First World War:

> As a young boy I delighted to visit City churches, especially on a Sunday evening when single bells beat from moonlit steeples down gas-lit alleys, and choirboys would rush round corners through vestry archways ... It was always my hope on some dark night to find a church which had escaped all the guide books and was there still in its classic splendour, with candles reflected in polished oak and cedar, with a parson in a black gown and bands, a beadle and the court of a City Company, robed and carrying a mace and swords.

Betjeman's memories, both of the London of his childhood and later of Oxford, find an echo in Compton MacKenzie's 1914 novel *Sinister Street*, an evocative account of a boy growing up in England in the late 1890s and early 1900s. The hero Michael Fane grows up in Kensington in London, has to cope with a hateful nanny, spends holidays in Cornwall and discovers the delights of Anglo-Catholic religion at a church that is a thinly veiled portrayal of St Stephen's, Bournemouth. The central section of the novel is concerned with Fane's years at the University of Oxford, and we are given a vivid picture of the university culture of the time, when MacKenzie could confidently assert, 'the great point of Oxford, in fact the whole point of Oxford, is that there are no girls'. It is small wonder that Betjeman thought this picture of the development of a precocious boy into a sophisticated young man was one of the best novels from the best period of English novel writing.

During his years in Cloth Fair Betjeman loved the sense of life within the walled city where in medieval times the bells of 108 city churches rang out. Just round the corner was

Livery hall of the Stationers and Newspaper Makers. John Betjeman loved the City livery companies, 'all bumbledom and beadles', and cherished the link they represent with the traditional trades and guilds of the medieval city. The Company of Stationers and Newspaper Makers was originally formed in 1403 to regulate the production of books and writing materials and is the 47th Company in order of precedence. Set discreetly behind Ludgate Hill, reached from Ave Maria Lane, the hall is a collage of work from the seventeenth to the twentieth century. The livery hall is particularly fine and remains much as it would have looked in 1674. (Courtesy of the Worshipful Company of Stationers and Newspaper Makers)

Smithfield Meat Market with 'its cheerful Chaucerian characters and medieval looking hand barrows ... southward the City became a river port with wharves and cobbled quays and a smell of fish from Billingsgate where alleys plunged steeply to the river.' Betjeman felt that what made the City so different were its churches, still oases of calm and prayer in the twentieth century, but above all the City's distinctive feature was its secrecy. 'It is really a village of about 400 people who know each other and whose words are their bond. If they break their word they are out. All this secret life is sealed by those medieval guilds, the City Companies with their livery halls, bumbledom and beadles.'

But the City was only part of the London that Betjeman knew and loved. He also admired the other city, Westminster, which grew up around the abbey, built on an island in the River Thames by Edward the Confessor, rebuilt by Henry III and completed by Henry VII in Tudor Gothic with its spectacular fan vaulting. Westminster became the abode of royalty, boasting Whitehall Palace, St James's Palace and Buckingham Palace, and it still keeps itself aloof and separate from the Square Mile. John Betjeman loved the civic splendour created by John Nash with his grand scheme of Regent Street, Piccadilly Circus, Carlton House Terrace and Trafalgar Square. He wandered the streets of Belgravia, admired the villas of St John's Wood,

This delightful drawing by Geoffrey Fletcher in 1969 records an electric lamp standard near the Wallace Collection in Manchester Square, London, and is just the sort of often-overlooked detail that John Betjeman loved to notice. (© Estate of Geoffrey Fletcher)

campaigned for Holy Trinity Sloane Square, St Mary-le-Strand and the Grosvenor Chapel, responded to the romance of the River Thames, the Isle of Dogs, Rotherhithe, all the way downstream to Chelsea, and defended the many fine bridges that cross the river, especially Tower Bridge, the Albert Suspension Bridge and Hammersmith Bridge.

Chelsea was a favourite area because Betjeman had known it since 1917 when his parents moved there. As always, it was the people who made a strong impression on him.

> When I first came to Chelsea as a youth there were a lot of characters about and it was people who were more prominent than buildings. There were still people who had been patted on the head as children by Carlyle. Lawrence Street was a haunted place because of the murder at the Cross Keys Public House: Radnor Street was a slum.

The River Thames here is a reminder of the Chelsea of James McNeill Whistler (1834–1903), and should be seen on a sultry afternoon with the pale early evening sun shining on the oily river, framed by the Albert Bridge. Then there were all the villages of outer London, which have become suburbs, despised by many but much loved by Betjeman, especially those to the west of London that comprise the old county of Middlesex, celebrated by Betjeman in numerous poems and prose pieces and, above all, in his TV programme of 1972 *Metro-Land* (see chapter four). Betjeman quite simply loved London in all its guises, and especially those forgotten or hidden corners that reminded him of the old London of his childhood.

Let's leave John Betjeman walking round his beloved City of London, as described by his friend Tom Driberg in January 1961. The two men started from Betjeman's flat in Cloth Fair, looking into St Bartholomew's Hospital with its splendid Hogarthian staircase, passing St Sepulchre's Church, the largest parish church in the City, rebuilt after the Great

Above: The Athenaeum Club and Lower Regent Street. John Betjeman belonged to the Garrick Club and the Athenaeum, and liked nothing better than dropping in at lunchtime for a dozen oysters and half a bottle of champagne. The Athenaeum, on the corner of Pall Mall and Lower Regent Street, was founded by John Wilson Crocker, Secretary of the Admiralty, in 1824 as a club for literary, scientific and artistic gentlemen, and has numbered Macaulay, Trollope, Matthew Arnold, Thakeray and Dickens among its members. The clubhouse was designed by Decimus Burton and sports a statue of Pallas Athene over the entrance portico. (Courtesy of the Athenaeum, Pall Mall, London)

Left: St Mary le Strand, London. This fine church, sitting on an island amid the London traffic, was a favourite of John Betjeman's. (Pen and ink drawing by Geoffrey Fletcher; © Estate of Geoffrey Fletcher)

Right: John Betjeman was part of a campaign, inaugurated by the then rector, Edward Thompson, to raise £400,000 to clean and restore this church, by James Gibbs, which sits on an island in the middle of the eastern end of the Strand. He described the interior as a 'baroque paradise' and wrote this poem about the church as part of the fundraising campaign. The church was restored, but today, because of the traffic thundering past on both sides, its future is uncertain.

Below: *The Adam and Eve: Old Chelsea* (1879) by James Whistler. This etching shows the range of old buildings along the River Thames at Chelsea, with the Adam and Eve tavern and the tower of Chelsea Old Church in the background. John Betjeman moved to Chelsea (No. 29 Radnor Walk) in 1973 to be near to his long-standing friend and companion Elizabeth Cavendish. (Wikimedia Commons)

Sir JOHN BETJEMAN

29, RADNOR WALK,
LONDON, SW3 4BP.

ST. MARY~LE~STRAND

Shall we give Gibbs the go by
Great Gibbs of Aberdeen,
Who gave the town of Cambridge
Its Senate House serene;
And every son of Oxford
Can recognise he's home
When he sees upon the skyline
The Radcliffe's mothering dome.
Placid above the chimney pots
His sculptured steeples soar.
Windowless he designs his walls
Above the traffic's roar.
Whenever you put stone on stone
You edified the scene.
Your chaste baroque was on its own,
Great Gibbs of Aberdeen
A Tory and a Catholic
There's nothing quite so grand
As the baroque of your Chapel
Of St. Mary in the Strand.

© St. Mary-le-Strand

Fire of London, and the drinking fountain on Holborn Viaduct, erected in 1859 by the Metropolitan Drinking Fountain Association, then on past the Old Bailey and the local pub The Magpie and Stump, on downwards, the City skyline a riot of cubes and towers, into Blackfriars Lane where you can still see the steeples of St Martin's and St Bride's as Christopher Wren meant them to be seen. Down a narrow lane the two travellers come upon Apothecaries Hall, the seventeenth-century buildings set around a secluded courtyard. At the busy Blackfriars Junction is the Black Friar public house, an art nouveau survival with mosaic panels and elaborate bronze reliefs of the monks whose monastery gives its name to this area, all shown quaffing ale and made by Henry Poole RA. On they go past Blackfriars station, now completely rebuilt, past the Mermaid Theatre, brainchild of the actor Bernard Miles and now a conference centre, down Upper Thames Street, the Billingsgate Fish Market, which moved out in 1982 to the Isle of Dogs, past St James Garlickhythe, Vintners' Hall, the towering brick sides of Canon Street station, past incense-laden St Magnus the Martyr, and in the early evening dusk to Leadenhall Market through homeward-bound crowds of commuters, finally calling in at St Mary-at-Hill before returning to Cloth Fair for a much needed glass of champagne, secure in the knowledge that this place is home and that the bells will soon be ringing to signal the start of evensong in nearby St Bartholomew the Great.

The Railways

Perhaps my earliest memory as a three-year-old child is of being taken by my grandfather to the railway bridge at Wolvercote when we were living in north Oxford. At that point the steam-hauled trains running north or north-west to Birmingham or Worcester would have gathered speed heading out of Oxford station and as they passed under the bridge, whistles blowing shrilly, the smoke and steam from the engine would billow up and over the parapet, completely enveloping us as we stood there. My brother and I would hide inside my grandfather's overcoat as the smoke swirled around us, then peep over the bridge to watch the express train receding into the distance.

So began my love of trains and railways, fed by our holiday train journeys to the West Country from Paddington station and later by family trips to Scotland and the Orkney Islands, which always began by taking the night-time sleeper train from London to Inverness, and latterly the Motorail to Perth. The excitement of getting into our sleeping cabin in London, drawing down the blind, travelling through the night snug in our berths, traversing the Forth Bridge in the early morning and arriving in the heart of the Highlands surrounded by mountains, forests and peaty rivers, is a sensation that has not diminished with the passing years. Like John Betjeman, I too as a teenager enjoyed exploring London's mainline stations and travelling on the London Underground, the earliest system of its kind in the world. I too, like John Betjeman before me, enjoyed journeys into London or out into 'Beechy Bucks' on the Metropolitan Line, part of the Metropolitan Railway that ran the world's first underground trains between Paddington and Farringdon in 1863.

*****

Paddington station, designed by Isambard Kingdom Brunel in 1838, was familiar to John Betjeman because of his schooldays at Marlborough and later when he lived at Uffington. He admired the genius of Brunel and thought the Great Western Railway the best in the world. Brunel built 'an aisled cathedral in a cutting ... The cutting is roofed over. Pillars of cast iron support a triple roof of wrought iron and glass ... A fourth aisle was added to the north side in 1916'. (John Betjeman, *London's Historic Railway Stations*, 1972). On Platform 1 there hangs the famous clock, and beside it the magnificent First World War memorial by Charles Sargeant Jagger. (Photography by John Gay; © Historic England Archive)

In his travels around London John Betjeman and his friend Ronnie Wright made extensive use of the Underground system. In his school holidays he and Ronnie travelled to every station on the network, and the Underground map became firmly imprinted on his mind. He felt the line with the most dominating personality was the Metropolitan Line because it had started in the age of steam, and some of the stations still bore signs of this steam heritage, with their smoke blackened bricks and gaslights, stations such as Bayswater, Notting Hill Gate, Euston Square and Swiss Cottage. 'The Metropolitan stretched its tentacles round the Inner Circle to Mansion House and South Kensington, over the Great Western to Hammersmith, eastward to Whitechapel and it even had running powers over the London and South Western to Richmond.'

The Metropolitan, City and South London, Central London, Bakerloo and other lines took Betjeman to the mainline railway stations, which form a kind of ring around inner London and connect the capital to all corners of Britain. Betjeman was, as Jonathan Glancey has said, 'a lifelong railway enthusiast, not one who stood with duffle bag taking down the numbers of locomotives, but a poet who loved railways from the bottom his heart'. He loved trains not just for themselves, but because they were a wonderful way of travelling through Britain and looking out, without having to drive, at ever-changing townscapes and countryside. He liked the romance of steam locomotives and the curious byways of Britain's railways. He liked to imagine himself working as a stationmaster or booking clerk at some obscure rural outpost. A number of his best poems are inspired by railway stations or railway journeys. Above all, Betjeman loved most of the mainline London stations, especially Gothic St Pancras, Perpendicular Liverpool Street, classical Paddington and Renaissance Charing Cross, but definitely not the 'soulless' concrete cavern of the modern Euston, which replaced the glorious Great Hall by Philip Hardwick and the imposing Doric Arch, so criminally destroyed in 1961, in spite of Betjeman's campaigning.

Betjeman saw a distinct similarity between churches and railway stations. He wrote an extended article on London's railway stations for a book about London called *Flower of Cities* (1949), which began:

Above left: John Betjeman remembered travelling around parts of the London Underground railway system when trains were steam hauled, and celebrated this in his poetry. In the 1950s and '60s there were a number of steam-hauled rail tours, but this event on 9 September 1961 was London Transport's 'Farewell to Steam'. The train ran from Baker Street to Amersham and back, and was steam hauled from Rickmansworth to Amersham. Tickets cost 6s and included a commemorative leaflet and route map. In 1973 John Betjeman gave expression to his fondness for the Metropolitan Railway in his BBC film *Metro-Land*.

Above right: On the final day of electric locomotive and steam-hauled trains on the Metropolitan Line the platforms at Rickmansworth were crowded with enthusiasts as Electric Loco No. 18, *Michael Faraday*, pulls the train from Baker Street into the platform. Metropolitan tank engine No. 42070 then took the train on to Amersham. The souvenir ticket was 6s for the return journey.

> The study of railway stations is something like the study of churches... For piscina, read cast-iron lamp bracket: for arcading read girder construction: for transepts, read waiting rooms: for hangings, read tin advertisements. Then with very little practice anyone with an eye for detail can date the objects inspected.

Betjeman saw the big termini as the cathedrals of the railway age, and the finest of all was St Pancras, built in the Gothic style by the Midland Railway in 1868, with its enormous iron and glass roof designed by the civil engineer William Barlow. In front of this are the booking hall, offices and hotel, designed by Sir George Gilbert Scott, with their picturesque clock tower, rows of middle-pointed windows, chimney pots and gently curving façade. It is an iconic feature of the London skyline, cathedral-like in its proportions, and thanks to Betjeman's campaigning with many others it was saved from demolition in the 1960s.

Betjeman was fascinated by the history of the railways in Britain, the particular characteristics of each railway company, their pride in their distinctive liveries, their rivalries and how they had developed. On his travels he took with him his copy of

Above left: Waterloo station wasn't one of John Betjeman's favourite stations, but he would have loved these domed payboxes in the Windsor Bar there. The space is now a branch of Foyle's Bookshop, but the cashiers' kiosks have survived and are incorporated in the store. (Photograph by John Gay; © Historic England Archive)

Above right: Liverpool Street station. The piers of the double-aisled canopy give the station a cathedral-like feel, as John Betjeman noted in his book *London's Historic Railway Stations*. The Gothic interior of the station 'rewards the railway antiquarian with startling features'. (Photograph by John Gay; © Historic England Archive)

Bradshaw's Guide and enjoyed plotting imaginary journeys around the country. He liked the tin advertisements for Mazawattee Tea or Dr J. Collis Browne's Chlorodyne on station walls, and the station waiting rooms with coal fires blazing away in Gothic grates, a large mahogany table in the middle and horse-hair benches and chairs around the walls.

> Think yourself back into that waiting-room and learn with me the first lesson the railway teaches us – to pay a proper respect to the past. Railways were built to last. None of your discarding last year's model and buying this year's. That horse-hair seat has supported the Victorian bustle, the frock coat of the merchant going city-wards first-class, your father in his best sailor suit when he was being taken to the seaside, and now it is supporting you; and it's far from worn out. That platform has seen the last farewells of sons and parents, has watched the city man returning home to break the news to his wife that he's bankrupt, has watched his neighbour come in a new suit one morning and with a first-class, instead of a third-class, ticket. Turn from the human history to the history of stone and steam and iron. The railway station in the old days was a monument to science. Euston, whose fine Doric portico – one of London's noblest buildings – was the new gateway to the North; King's Cross whose simple outlines are a foretaste of all that is good in modern architecture; Temple Meads, Bristol, in the Tudor style, far from gimcrack, but cut out of local

Above left: St Pancras station, London. The terminus of the Midland Railway was purposely designed by George Gilbert Scott to contrast with its neighbour stations Euston and King's Cross. The magnificent train shed by William Henry Barlow was completed in 1868, and the hotel was opened in 1873. The clusters of pinnacles, chimney pots and clock tower and spire made it an exuberant addition to the London skyline. Threatened with demolition in the 1960s, John Betjeman campaigned vigorously with others to save it, and succeeded. It has been magnificently restored since then and is now a five-star hotel and a fitting arrival and departure point for the Eurostar trains to the Continent. (Photograph by John Gay; © Historic England Archive)

Above right: Statue of Sir John Betjeman in St Pancras station. There he stands, looking up at Barlow's wonderful train shed roof, on the concourse of St Pancras station, which he helped to save. The statue is a depiction of John Betjeman in bronze by the sculptor Martin Jennings. It was unveiled in November 2007 by John Betjeman's daughter, Candida Lycett Green, and Poet Laureate Andrew Motion to mark the opening of St Pancras International. (Courtesy of Wikimedia Commons)

stone; Newcastle Central station, a lovely classical building, and many a lesser station. I know little stations among the Shropshire hills built in a solid but picturesque Gothic style to tone in with the romantic scenery. I know of huge suburban stations which are dusty from disuse and full of top-hatted ghosts in the corners of echoing gas-lit booking halls. Best of all I know that station in Cornwall I loved as a boy, the oil lights, the smell of seaweed floating up the estuary, the rain-washed platform and the sparkling granite, and the hedges along the valleys around, soon to be heavy with blackberries.

(From 'Back to the Railway Carriage' by John Betjeman, *The Listener*, 28 March 1940)

3

The Shell Guides,
Piper and Pevsner

His friend John Sparrow understood that Betjeman's writing, both poetry and prose, was rooted in an appreciation of the human properties of place. 'For the landscape that most appeals to him is the inhabited landscape: he cannot see a place without seeing also the life that is lived in it, without becoming conscious of its human associations.' (*The Poetry of John Betjeman: Independent Essays,* 168)

When Betjeman was on a cruise around the Scottish Islands in 1959 he commented to John Smith, the founder of the Landmark Trust, when they landed on a deserted island with only birds in sight: 'I'm only interested in what Man has done.' (John Betjeman Letters, Vol 2, p. 156, ed. Candida Lycett Green, 1995)

The poet W. H. Auden, in his introduction to the American edition of Betjeman's collected poems *Slick But Not Streamlined* (1947), described Betjeman as a 'topophil', which he thought was a distinct form of landscape appreciation. 'It has little in common with nature love. Wild or unhumanised nature holds no charms for the average 'topophil' because it is lacking in history.'

Betjeman had grown up reading and using Victorian and Edwardian guidebooks, which focused on medieval architecture and were full of antiquarian lore and architectural terms. He nursed an ambition to write a series of guides that would focus instead on 'buildings in the landscape' and find the curious and unsung bits of England, especially 'the fast disappearing Georgian landscape of England, industrial towns, horrifying villas in overrated resorts'. Just as he liked the early railway stations, so he wanted to celebrate Georgian architecture at a time when such buildings were dismissed as mere dull square boxes. In similar vein he also wanted to include Victorian architecture, largely neglected or despised at that time.

Early in 1933 Betjeman suggested to Jack Beddington, the flamboyant Publicity Manager at Shell-Mex/BP, the idea of a series of guides to English counties, the *Shell Guides*, which would introduce the buildings and landscape of England to people who knew little or nothing about architecture. It is worth remembering just how novel it was in those days to look at one's own country instead of abroad.

However, there was a good growing interest in exploring and celebrating the glories of England, stimulated by the rise of motor car ownership, and given expression by the poet W. H. Auden in his book of 1936 *Look Stranger*, which included the poem:

The Church of St Winwallo in the pretty village of Landewednack, as recorded for John Betjeman's first *Shell Guide*, on Cornwall, published in 1934 by the Architectural Press. The lady in her Sunday best approaching the church gives a personal touch to the view of the medieval building.

> Look, stranger, on this island now
> The leaping light for your delight discovers,
> Stand stable here
> And silent be...

The poet suggests that we are all 'strangers' to our own island country, and invites us to move beyond our stereotypical prejudices to rediscover its beauties for ourselves. This impulse was very much a part of Betjeman's own mission, and it was his growing friendship with John Piper which encouraged Piper in the same direction.

Betjeman saw himself as a self-taught, practical man, conducting his research on location, not a professional art historian or desiccated antiquary. He loved to unearth the unconventional and unregarded among bits of architecture, places and people, and with his strong visual sense and lively imagination he could convert these experiences into memorable words. Alan Powers has commented: 'Betjeman was not a historian, but he understood architecture on many levels, above all in the way that places interact with our emotions.'

Mark Girouard quotes a review of his early book of poems, *Continual Dew*, in the *Architectural Review* in 1937:

> When he [John Betjeman] allows his love full play, even the bungalow, the revving sports car, the tough young gentleman from the RMC, even the suburban railway ... reveal ... a kind of unearthly beauty ... That awareness of what one is bound to call the divine in the banal...

This was the kind of inspiration and sensibility that animated the early *Shell Guides*, the first of which, *Cornwall*, written by Betjeman, appeared in 1934, priced at 2s 6d, with eccentric typography and quirky entries on Cornish pasties and fishing. As Timothy Mowl has said, 'To read a *Shell Guide* was to become an informed convert to architecture and breath a practical patriotism.' Betjeman's *Cornwall* was a shaky start, overly didactic and snobbish, but he learnt from Robert Byron's *Wiltshire*, with a gazetteer by Edith Oliver that was 'informed, allusive, engagingly devoted to the supernatural'. Betjeman wrote his second *Shell Guide*, this time to Devon, in 1936, and this is a much more assured production, full

Right: John Betjeman approached his friend Robert Byron, an established travel writer, for the second *Shell Guide* to be published, in 1935. His eccentric front cover is a densely packed photomontage, bringing together elements of the county, people, buildings and animals, all squashed together to suggest oddity and quaintness.

Below: John Betjeman commissioned John Piper to write the *Shell Guide to Oxfordshire*, which was published in 1938. Piper toured the county, making notes and drawings in his sketchbooks, and this method is reflected in the endpapers, which are collages of maps, notes and typography, giving a scrapbook effect. The guide celebrates deserted places and hidden gems, the small and neglected beauties of 'one of the most ordinary of the English counties'.

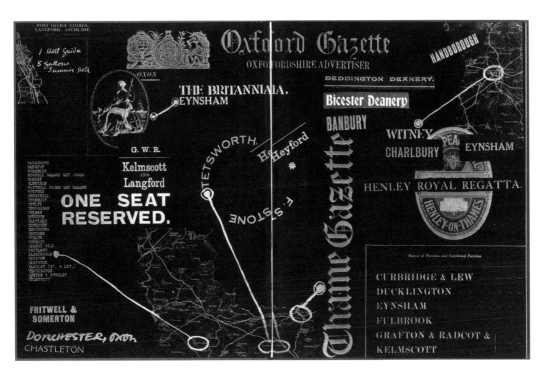

of fun, mystical whimsy and trenchant comment. Soon further guides to Northumberland, Dorset and Somerset were on the way. Through working on these guides Betjeman was introduced to the person who became one of his closest friends and collaborators, the artist John Piper (1903–92). The two men discovered that their vision of England chimed exactly,

John Piper, like John Betjeman, loved the unusual and unregarded sights in the English landscape, and here found a scarecrow full of character in an Oxfordshire field, which he included in his *Shell Guide to Oxon*. (© Tate)

St Katherine's, Chiselhampton, Oxfordshire. Standing on the edge of a small park is this delightful Georgian church of 1763, with a bell cote and clear glass windows. Inside are box pews, a Jacobean pulpit, west gallery, altar rails and wooden reredos. All unspoiled and lovingly preserved, thanks in part to the efforts of John Betjeman in 1952, when he wrote a poem supporting its restoration, 'Verses turned in aid of A Public Subscription towards the restoration of the Church of St Katherine Chiselhampton, [*sic*] Oxon.' (A photograph taken by John Piper when researching his *Shell Guide to Oxon*; © Tate)

and there was much cross-pollination of ideas on the work they both did for the *Shell Guides*. Indeed, Piper shared Betjeman's reservations about Nikolaus Pevsner's approach. He once remarked, 'Pevsner is very good at telling you everything about a place except what it's like.' Piper wrote the *Guide to Oxfordshire (Oxon)*, which is probably the best of the series. It was a revelation to Betjeman how Piper saw beauty in the most unlikely places. 'Piper opened up the gates of enjoyment, through which John Betjeman became the poet of reassurance, the open-minded observer of middle-class and working-class life' (Timothy Mowl). They later collaborated on the *Murray's Guides* to *Buckinghamshire* (1948) and *Berkshire* (1949), which showed how a combination of well-informed text and excellent photography (mainly by Piper) could be a winning combination, easily eclipsing the early *Buildings of England* series, written by Nikolaus Pevsner. Their collaboration was a success because 'the poet's eye fed on what was valued by the painter' (Anthony West). Indeed, as A. N. Wilson has observed, 'Piper found his own style and conviction by working with Betjeman on the *Shell Guides*: "I found I was English and Romantic".'

Two events in the 1930s were influential in creating the foundations of Betjeman's personal approach to topographical writing. The first was Betjeman's visit to Leeds when he was sent by the *Architectural Review* to report on the opening of E. Vincent Harris's new Civic Hall. Timothy Mowl has claimed that in the article he subsequently wrote for the *Review*, Betjeman discovered his distinctive voice. He realised that buildings can't be detached from topography, and that the most important part of a building's context is not just the physical locale but its place in the lives of actual people who live and work in and around it.

The other event occurred in 1939 when Betjeman and Piper visited the Hafod estate in Cardiganshire, a garden in the picturesque tradition created by Thomas Johnes in the Ystwyth Valley. Johnes was a cousin of Richard Payne Knight and a friend of Uvedale Price, both followers of the aesthetic ideal first introduced in 1782 by William Gilpin in his *Observations on the River Wye*. An earlier influence can be found in the writings of Joseph Addison in his influential book *Pleasures of the Imagination* (1712), in which he proposes that sight is the most important of the senses, and the greatest stimulus to imaginative thought.

Hafod, Uchtryd, west Wales. This wooded and landscaped estate in Ceredigion became in the eighteenth century a celebrated picturesque estate, created by Colonel Thomas Johnes between 1790 and 1810. The print by J. C. Stadler shows the house and countryside in 1795. (Courtesy of Wikimedia Commons)

By the pleasures of the imagination I mean only such pleasures as arise originally from sight, and that I divide these pleasures into two kinds – primary pleasures which proceed from such objects as are before our eyes: and those secondary pleasures which flow from the ideas of visible objects, when the objects are not actually before the eye, but are called up into our memories, or formed into agreeable visions of things that are either absent or fictitious.

(Joseph Addison, *The Spectator*, No. 277)

In the late eighteenth century rationalist ideas about aesthetics were being challenged by the belief that the experience of beauty was instinctual rather than rational. Characteristics of the picturesque were irregularity of form and colour with sudden variations and surprises allied to roughness and grandeur. The picturesque style emphasised the personal and the particular and used the power of memory and association to evoke feelings of wonder and romance in the viewer. At Hafod, Thomas Johnes had created a garden full of variety, startling vistas, 'a masterclass in the aesthetics of the beautiful and sublime.' Betjeman owned a folio book of etchings of Hafod, after watercolours made by John 'Warwick' Smith in 1797, and inspired by these John and Myfanwy Piper visited Hafod when holidaying in Wales in August 1939. Piper was profoundly affected by the remote and semi-derelict estate, and afterwards wrote enthusiastically to Betjeman about their visit.

Both Betjeman and Piper were strongly influenced by their visit to Hafod, and attracted to the picturesque style. In 1941 Piper wrote a patriotic wartime book called *British Romantic Artists*, which made connections between particular painters, geography and climate.

He wrote: 'Romantic art is the result of a vision that can see in things something significant beyond ordinary significance: something that for a moment seems to contain the whole world; and, when the moment is past, carries over some comment on life or experience besides the comment on appearances.' This realisation, which has echoes of Harry William's belief that the ordinary world is full of unimagined wonder, stimulated Piper to look at landscape with a fresh eye and encouraged his own painting in a more consciously romantic direction.

In his book *British Romantic Artists* he went on to trace the rise of the picturesque tradition in the art of J. W. M. Turner and William Gilpin, and concluded: 'They wanted to make landscape a means of reporting and recording, not places and things, but life.'

John Piper visited Hafod in 1939 and was profoundly influenced by what he saw. The visit moved him towards a picturesque and romantic approach to landscape and buildings. (Photograph taken by John Piper; © Tate)

The painting captures the interior of St James's Church, Great Packington, Warwickshire, built by Joseph Bonomi in 1789–90 and regarded as the most important eighteenth-century church in England. A classic mausoleum design with semicircular windows and pepper-pot towers at the four corners. (From one of John Piper's sketchbooks containing mostly pencil sketches of churches and townscapes; ©Tate)

The handsome village of Folkingham, Lincolnshire, on a hillside with an old coaching inn and church with good rood screen and lofty Perpendicular tower – a local landmark. At some distance stands the 'House of Correction', 1825, by Bryan Browning, with its forbidding classical front, in fact the original gatehouse. Piper became a keen photographer, recording the buildings and places he visited on his travels around the country, making meticulous notes and drawings in the sketchbooks that accompanied him. (Photograph by John Piper; © Tate)

St George's, Goltho, Lincolnshire. A tiny church in a remote setting in a field with the remains of the local family mansion. An early example of a seventeenth-century, brick-built church, but sadly neglected. (Photograph by John Piper; © Tate)

Gilpin defined the picturesque as 'that kind of beauty which is agreeable in a picture', and his contemporary Uvedale Price wrote of finding beauty and interest 'where a common eye sees nothing but ruts and rubbish'.

Betjeman was sharing a similar vision when he wrote his wartime book *English Cities and Small Towns*, published in 1943. This was part of his realignment towards a vision of England where the Nazi spirit of totalitarian modernism was the enemy of what England stood for. Betjeman writes in his introduction:

Not until you have been away from it, as has the author of this book for more than a year, do you realise how beautiful is the meanest English town. Not the most magnificent scenery, misty mountains, raging seas, desert sunsets, or groves of orange can compensate for the loss of the Corn Exchange, the doctor's house, tennis in suburban gardens, the bank and the bank-manager's house, the rural garages, the arid municipal park, the church clock and the Jubilee drinking fountain.

And he goes on:

When exploring, for the first time, one of these pockets of English history, local pride and marked character, the approach I like to make is by railway, for from the railway line you get an impression of the surrounding country, undisturbed by the adjuncts of a main road ... A road cuts for a few hundred yards through new brick villas to the heart of the old town. This road is probably called 'Station Row', the name in white on a blue tin background affixed to the bright red wall of the side of a house. The villas are of a type not later than 1910, for few railway stations were built after that date ... They each have trim little gardens with privet hedges and squeaking cast iron gates painted green or plum.

This attraction to the local, the vernacular, and the unregarded, as Mark Girouard puts it, 'the divine in the banal', was echoed in the direction which Piper's painting had taken, towards a more romantic Englishness after his period of abstractionism. Indeed, Geoffrey Grigson criticised Piper's liking for the romantic and picturesque as 'Betjemanism in paint.'

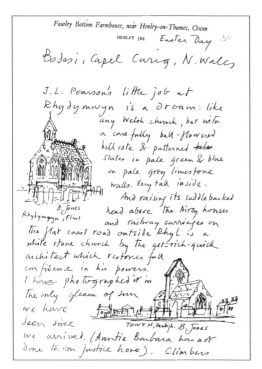

Above left: Letter from John Piper to John Betjeman. Piper, like Betjeman, filled his letters with little drawings in pen and ink. Here he writes from North Wales on Easter Day 1950, describing churches at Rhydymwyn and Towyn.

Above right: A pen and ink drawing of the fine medieval St Botolph Church in the remote spot of Wardley, Rutland. Very possibly drawn by John Betjeman, showing an identical view to the black-and-white photograph by Edwin Smith in the *Shell Guide to Rutland*, 1963. The rear section of this John Piper notebook is full of drawings and notes of places and churches in a hand that is not Piper's. The handwriting is more untidy and the drawing less controlled, making it likely that Piper had given Betjeman one of his sketchbooks while they were touring Rutland together. (© Tate)

Sir Simon Jenkins, who knew John Betjeman well and whose book *England's Thousand Best Churches* (1999) is his personal tribute to him, feels that Betjeman always saw buildings and streetscapes as pictures. Betjeman mentions in *Summoned by Bells* that as a boy he saw Frank Bramley's painting *The Hopeless Dawn* in the Tate Gallery in London and was captivated by the genre of Victorian narrative painting in which within each picture there is a story to uncover. Simon Jenkins is convinced that Betjeman looked at buildings in the same way, imagining the stories they enshrined and wanting to know about the histories of the people who inhabited the 'picture' he saw in front of him. This narrative approach to the built environment has echoes of the Platonic way of 'seeing' that I mentioned in the introduction, with its emphasis on being a participant rather than a spectator.

Because of Betjeman's and Piper's emotional approach to architecture and landscape they focused on the particular and the domestic. Betjeman tried in his *Shell Guides* and *Collins Guide to English Parish Churches* to avoid the technicalities of the old guidebooks and to make churches feel as warm and familiar as 'a house that has been lived in for generations'. Churches, he said, are not backwaters but strongholds, focal points of village culture where music has flourished and where there is an art gallery in glass, wall painting and stone carving – a theatre where rituals acted out at the altar spilled over into entertainments in the market square.

This romantic and emotional approach to buildings was diametrically opposed to the outlook of Professor Nikolaus Pevsner. His method was determinedly scientific, 'employing the rationalism of a foreigner evaluating a heritage not his own', as Alexandra Harris has observed. (*Romantic Moderns*, Thames and Hudson, 2015)

Betjeman's antipathy to Pevsner originated in his resentment that Pevsner had moved into what he regarded as 'his' territory, teaching the English about themselves, but doing so in a way that Betjeman regarded as pedantic, dry and sterile. Betjeman favoured taste over scholarship and felt it was better to be discerning rather than bookish, intuitive rather than diligent. As John Summerson, the art historian, remarked: 'John Betjeman's way of talking about architecture was a sort of deliberate amateurism. ... When he writes about buildings, he does not write about them as form ... but as evocation.' And Summerson reflects, 'What he [John Betjeman] did not like was illumination of the obscure by art historians ... The Pevsner approach was like installing a system of floodlights in a twilight landscape.' (Quoted in *John Betjeman Letters*, ed. by Candida Lycett Green, Vol. 2, p. 140.)

It is instructive to compare the published corpus of Betjeman's radio talks with those given by Pevsner. Between 1932 and 1978 Betjeman made over 300 radio broadcasts, and between 1945 and 1977 Pevsner made around 120 broadcasts on radio and television. Both men have been beautifully anthologised by Stephen Games, in his edition on Pevsner, *The Complete Broadcast Talks 1945–1977* (Ashgate, 2014) and on Betjeman, *Trains and Buttered Toast* (John Murray, 2006). From these books Pevsner emerges as precise, scholarly and pedantic, with, perhaps predictably, a strongly Germanic, even nationalistic, outlook, especially when defending the modern movement in architecture. There are occasional references to Betjeman, usually critical, as well as negative comments about Betjeman's hero Sir Ninian Comper. Betjeman is bracketed with Paul Nash and John Piper in liking 'bollards, non-conformist chapels, and seaside seats, and cottages, and Victorian pubs and playbills and so on ... They still feel that a liking for Blandford or the High at Oxford or indeed William Butterfield must exclude a liking for the twentieth century [style in] architecture.'

Games comments that when Pevsner tried to adopt a more folksy, conversational or anecdotal tone, in imitation of Betjeman's style, 'he was too aloof to pull this off convincingly', and merely succeeded in muddling the listener with unhelpful diversions.

When analysing Betjeman's output Games says that not only was Betjeman more versatile and able to talk extempore, with the added virtue of a satirical sense of humour, but also the range and outlook of the talks were distinctive:

> Many of his most brilliant talks concern the way in which places are seen. He spoke about the impact of light and shade, the effect of rain, the view from a train window, the profound emotion of suddenly seeing the sea. He also insisted, in defiance of the new profession of architectural historians, that buildings were inseparable from those who lived in them.

Betjeman was not an immediate success on the radio. At first he thought the radio was vulgar, and his interest in the outré and the eccentric gained him the reputation of being a crank. His slightly camp Oxford accent didn't help either. But through his work for the

West of England service he began to find his voice, and during the Second World War years his sympathies and outlook broadened considerably. He became the mouthpiece for the common man, speaking out against philistinism and fighting for an England he felt was imperilled by bureaucrats and soulless officialdom.

As Games says, 'Unlike those architectural historians whom he regarded as rivals and pedants (such as Pevsner), Betjeman liked to present himself as a practical man. He was self-taught rather than academic.' This celebration of the eclectic and the undiscovered, the ability to focus on the ordinary and the everyday in a personal and rhapsodic style, as well as his frank expression of his inner life and spiritual longings, was all in complete contrast to the restrained, intellectual and analytical style of Pevsner's talks on architecture and his approach to communicating the subject to his audience, which always sounded like the university lecture room in which he was clearly much more at home.

While Pevsner could appreciate Betjeman's strengths and recognise him as someone to whom architecture was a joy, 'arousing a personal response which he delighted to hand on to others' (Susan Harries, *Nikolaus Pevsner: The Life: Chatto and Windus*, 2011), the conflict between the two men really came into the open in an exchange of letters between them in the *Times Literary Supplement* in 1948 about a book on Georgian churches. The exchange culminated in Betjeman writing: 'So long as he [Pevsner] ... puts style and names of architects as a consideration before worship and the use of the eye for beauty, we will obviously never agree about the quality and interest of a church.' Later on, Pevsner really caught Betjeman in a tender place when he chose to criticise one of Betjeman's heroes, the architect John Ninian Comper.

Comper (1864–1960) was a Scottish-born architect, one of the last who worked in the Gothic Revival tradition. He had been articled to Charles Eamer Kempe, and then in 1883 to George Frederick Bodley and Thomas Garner. In the early part of his career he followed in the footsteps of A. W. N. Pugin, insisting on closing off the chancel with a screen, as at St Cyprian's, Clarence Gate, in London; however, after a visit to Rome in 1904 he came to see that other ways of arranging the sacred space were valid, and that the fourth-century church plan, which set the altar forward from the east end and brought the action of the Mass into the middle of the worshipping community, had much to commend it. His church of St Philip's, Cosham, incorporated these new ideas: the whole airy space focused on the altar, brought forward and set under a baldachino of burnished gold.

Sir John Ninian Comper (1864–1960) was a Scottish-born architect, one of the last of those to design in the Gothic Revival style. His work had largely been overlooked until championed by John Betjeman, who had met him in the 1930s. He had admired Comper's work since his childhood encounter with his altars in Blisland Church in Cornwall.

Comper designed a number of churches in a similar style, a fusion of Gothic, classical and baroque called 'Unity by Inclusion'. His long life thus linked the architecture of the High Victorian ritualist revival with the liturgical changes of the 1950s and '60s, by which time Comper's work was regarded as old-fashioned, mannered and overly ornate.

Betjeman first met Comper in 1937, when he was seventy-three and Betjeman thirty-one, and the two men struck up an unlikely friendship. Starting with his article in the *Architectural Review* of 1939, 'A Note on J. N. Comper: Heir to Butterfield and Bodley', Betjeman became Comper's champion. This provoked Pevsner to criticise Comper for mixing together different styles, and he took every opportunity in the *Buildings of England* series to denigrate and dismiss Comper's work. Comper believed that church design should always support the liturgy and inspire reverence. He designed from the altar outwards and his buildings glowed with gilt altars, baldachinos, colouring on wood, stone and ceiling, and stained glass in the windows. In his 1947 pamphlet *Of The Atmosphere of a Church*, he wrote: 'The purpose of a church is not to express the age in which it was built or the individuality of its designer. Its purpose is to move to worship, to bring a man to his knees, to refresh his soul in a weary land.'

These are sentiments with which Betjeman profoundly agreed, and he admired Comper's devotion to the fusion of beauty and holiness. He frequently took people to visit St Mary Magdalene's Church at Paddington, a fine church by G. E. Street, with its crypt Chapel of St Sepulchre, lavishly decorated by Comper. Then he would take them on to St Cyprian's, Clarence Gate, and show them photos of St Mary's, Wellingborough.

Comper himself wrote of St Cyprian's, Clarence Gate, which is an evocation of a fifteenth-century parish church:

> The whole church has become a lantern and the altar is the flame within it. The high chancel and the side chancels are separated from the nave and from each other by coloured and guilded screens which, seen against the silver and jewels of the painted glass, greatly enrich the beauty of the altar but obstruct the view of it no more than a lantern hides the light it is made to contain.

However, to Pevsner, with his firm belief in the values of modernism, Comper's approach was both anachronistic, and smacked of pastiche. For Pevsner, 'the church architect had to be able to promote worship in a manner that was appropriate to his own times, not by evoking the atmosphere of an age of faith that was gone, and certainly not by picking and mixing from the styles of different ages.' (Susan Harries, *Nikolaus Pevsner, The Life*, Chatto and Windus, 2011, p. 543)

He thought Betjeman's admiration for Comper was the result of confounding aesthetic with religious emotions, and he said so publicly in his *Buildings of England* volume on *London*. The fusing of religious and aesthetic emotions in approaching ecclesiastical architecture was just what Betjeman thought was essential for a full appreciation of the building, so this criticism aimed at the very heart of Betjeman's creed, and his dislike of Pevsner intensified thereafter. In 1982, in the last two years of his life, Betjeman said, 'Why is it that when you've read what Pevsner has to say about a building, you never want to look at that building ever again?'

In the end, for all their shared love of architecture, the two men, John Betjeman and Nikolaus Pevsner, were very different personalities and approached their subject from different directions. In reality there is room for both approaches, the personal and the

Above left: St Cyprian's, Clarence Gate, London. Designed by J. N. Comper in 1903, the brick buttressed exterior contrasts with the glowing interior. A wide nave with a gilded screen and loft, all leading the eye to the altar. Pevsner was dismissive of this church in his *Buildings of England* volume, which angered John Betjeman and contributed to their estrangement.

Above right: Pusey House Chapel, St Giles, Oxford. The glittering ciborium is by John Ninian Comper, who also designed the east window above.

academic, as Betjeman reluctantly acknowledged. But he feared that Pevsner's 'stripped' approach to architecture was in fact a loveless one, while he himself loved context, association and allusion, and an emphasis on people, habits and rituals that brought buildings and their contents to life. It was this pleasure in the personal and peculiar, as well as in the architectural elements of landscape and places, that drew Betjeman and John Piper together. Betjeman felt that Piper had enlarged our visual sense, made us look at things a second time, and brought the overlooked parts of our towns and villages to life. He was profoundly influenced by his long friendship with Piper, which expanded his own visual sensibility:

> I come to you fresh from Evensong with my outlook widened. Architecture has a wider meaning than that which is commonly given to it. For architecture means not a house, or a single building, or a church, or Sir Herbert Baker, or the glass at Chartres, but your surroundings: not a town or a street, but our whole overpopulated island. It is concerned with where we eat, work, sleep, play, congregate, escape. It is our background...

4
The Television Years: Metro-land and Norfolk

I grew up in Metro-land. My parents moved to Pinner, in Middlesex, in 1951, when my brother and I were four years old. They were following the aspirational dream of those immediate post-war years and moving out of cramped central London into suburbia, where there was more space, fresh air, trees and fields, and a community to which they could belong. So all my formative years, up to university and beyond, were spent in the quiet, ordered suburban world of North West London. In those early days there were still leafy lanes and small shops, and the main roads were lined with mature trees. Pinner High Street climbed picturesquely up its hill with old buildings still surviving, including the Old Oak Tea Rooms and the Queen's Head public house. Crowning the hill, and surrounded by more ancient cottages, was the parish church dedicated to St John the Baptist, a typical Middlesex church with a fine flint-dressed tower, and in the churchyard the obelisk erected by John Claudius Loudon, of gardening fame, to his parents in 1843, with a sarcophagus sticking out halfway up. In the 1950s traffic was relatively light and most people used bicycles, buses and trains to get around. From Pinner we took the Metropolitan Line up to London or out to Amersham and the Chiltern Hills. During the 1960s, when we owned a car, a smart Morris Oxford, we were driven further afield to explore the further reaches of Metro-land and to travel via Motorail up to Scotland for our summer holidays. But in my earlier years it is outings to places like Harrow-on-the-Hill that I remember best. Taking the train to Harrow station, we would climb the steep footpath up to the top of Harrow Hill and visit the medieval parish church of St Mary, perched on the top, with its splendid vistas across Middlesex and an old bench on which we could sit and catch our breath. The church is the highest point in Middlesex, where Lord Byron used to sit on his favourite tombstone (the Peachey Tomb) as a Harrow schoolboy, daydreaming his afternoons away. 'Harrow village', said John Betjeman in his *Collins Guide to English Parish Churches*, 'preserves its hilltop quiet, looking from its elmy height over miles of roof and railway.' After a visit to the church we would wander down the main street, with its small shops serving the needs of Harrow School, and have afternoon tea in the local tea shop, before wending our way down the path in the late afternoon sunshine to Harrow station and the train home.

Pinner High Street, lined with some pretty half-timbered houses, leads up the hill past the Queen's Head public house to Georgian brick houses that surround the church. This view, filled with the stalls and roundabouts of the annual Charter Fair, features in John Betjeman's film *Metro-Land*. (Courtesy of Stuart Vallis)

The view from the top of Harrow Hill stretches for many miles across suburbia, but once Harrow was just a small town surrounded by trees, until the famous school grew to prominence in the mid-nineteenth century. With the establishment of the London to Birmingham Railway in the 1830s, and then the extension of the Metropolitan Line in 1880, the town expanded at the bottom of the hill, leaving the area around the church as an oasis of tranquillity. The print by W. Radcliffe shows an early steam train in 1840 with Harrow Hill and church in the background.

Above: A view from Harrow-on-the-Hill over the surrounding countryside. In the foreground is the Peachey tomb on which Byron sat as he daydreamed away his afternoons as a Harrow schoolboy. He recorded the spot in his 'Lines Written Beneath an Elm in the Churchyard of Harrow'. The view from the tower of St Mary's Church is said to take in thirteen counties. (Courtesy of Stuart Vallis)

Left: Harrow School was founded in 1572 by John Lyon of Harrow and expanded considerably in the Victorian era. It is now a leading independent boys' school and was a favourite of John Betjeman's, who liked to imagine he had been a pupil there. The school buildings line the main street through the village. (Courtesy of Stuart Vallis)

Metro-land

John Betjeman had been honing his television skills since he first tried the medium with the redoubtable BBC producer Mary Adams in 1937 at Alexandra Palace. After the end of the Second World War George Barnes, Head of Television in the 1950s and who was to become a good friend, encouraged him to try television work again. He had been making a series of twenty-six short films produced by Shell called *Discovering Britain*, and Barnes was keen to lure him back to the BBC. Unconstrained by government-sponsored documentaries he became a TV natural, communicating his passion with the flair and the tricks of a born performer.

Because he loved railways, he made numerous films for British Transport Films including *Railways for Ever* in 1968. In it he said:

> I am told that in the mid-seventies we will have trains going at 150 miles per hour or more, but I don't think it's the speed that matters. It's the release from tension and the thrill of seeing real country which you do from the trains. And for some of us there will always remain memories of the hiss of steam, the sudden roar, the triumphant scream of the whistle, smuts and the grimy majesty of the whole thing ... Ah yes, Railways For Ever.
>
> (Quoted in John Betjeman's Coming Home, Methuen, 1997, p. 373)

Throughout the 1960s Betjeman made nearly a hundred film and TV appearances, memorably collaborating with the BBC producer Kenneth Savidge on *An ABC of Churches*, with a commentary, often in verse, by Betjeman. He took great pains over every aspect of production but also managed to make the whole enterprise fun. He got to know the TV crews, kept everybody in good spirits with his jokes and laughter, and enjoyed sneaking off to the pub with the drivers.

In December 1972 Betjeman starred in a two-part television film called *Thank God It's Sunday*, directed by Jonathan Stedall, which was a tongue-in-cheek commentary on how ordinary people spent their Sundays in the latter part of the twentieth century. Stedall had first got to know Betjeman in the early 1960s when he was working for Television Wales and the West and made a series of films about West Country towns with Betjeman. The two men became friends and Stedall went on to make a number of films with Betjeman, including *Thank God It's Sunday* (1972), *Summoned by Bells* (1976) and *Time with Betjeman* (1981–82). Stedall remembers particularly the final scene of *Thank God It's Sunday*, in which an elderly man is seen wandering alone along an almost deserted Sussex beach while Betjeman's commentary meditates on the essential loneliness of life and the uncertainty of what awaits us in the hereafter. He ends, 'Faith, hope, charity ... Oh give me hope.'

It was the following year that saw the finest of Betjeman's television films, *Metro-Land*, first screened in February 1973. Betjeman had long felt nostalgic for the lost delights of rural Middlesex. In spite of Heathrow Airport, the reservoirs and the factories, there were many unspoiled corners, old churches, weatherboarded cottages and brick mansions in places like Perivale, Stanwell and South Mimms. Betjeman's favourite churches were St Mary's at Harefield, crammed with a splendid gallery of monuments from the fifteenth to the end of the eighteenth centuries, and in the east All Hallows', Tottenham, enlarged by William Butterfield, who lies buried in the churchyard. Another much-loved building was the Great

Above left: John Betjeman in 1981, with John and Myfanwy Piper and Jonathan Stedall, outside St Mary's, Harefield, Middlesex. (Courtesy of Jonathan Stedall)

Above right: An unlikely survivor of medieval Middlesex. This exceptional tithe barn at Harmondsworth was rescued by English Heritage after years of neglect. In 1973 John Betjeman visited the barn with Simon Jenkins and surreptitiously crawled in through stacks of hay to have a look. He called it 'The Cathedral of Middlesex'. (Courtesy of Jonathan Gibson/Country Life Picture Library)

Tithe Barn at Harmondsworth, dating from the fourteenth century. Sir Simon Jenkins remembers a visit with Betjeman in 1970 when they crawled in through locked doors and up through the hay to admire the magnificent vaulted roof. Jenkins remembers Betjeman carrying vestiges of hay on his suit for the rest of the day, murmuring, 'Ah, Harmondsworth hay.' Middlesex is mentioned frequently in Betjeman's poetry, with three poems about the Metropolitan Line in his 1954 collection *A Few Late Chrysanthemums* – 'Harrow-on-the-Hill', 'Middlesex' and 'The Metropolitan Railway'. He had a particular fondness for Harrow School and liked to imagine that he had been a schoolboy there rather than at Marlborough College, of which he retained very mixed memories. Harrow-on-the-Hill features often in his poetry and in 1973 he did a radio broadcast about Harrow School songs. But it was the whole of Metro-land that captured Betjeman's imagination. In a book called *Metro Memories* (1977), Dennis Edwards and Ron Pigram described its appeal:

> The image of Metro-land is as identifiable with the period between the two world wars as char-a-bancs, school treats and jazz. To most people who lived around London in those days it meant many things – most of them associated with the countryside and fresh air – and was so intense that Metro-land has come to us, almost fifty years on, as more than nostalgia.

A 1914 London Underground poster advertising the peace and fresh air of Metro-land, which was marketed by the Metropolitan Railway as a place of idyllic cottages and wild flowers. (Courtesy of Lordprice Collection/Alamy Stock Photo)

The term 'Metro-land' came into use as a means of promoting passenger traffic to that part of Middlesex, the Buckinghamshire Chilterns and the Vale of Aylesbury through which the Metropolitan Railway had built its lines.

During the 1920s and '30s campaigns were launched to persuade Londoners to abandon the grime of cramped conditions in central London for homes in leafy countryside. The Metropolitan Railway owned large amounts of surplus land and built new homes for Londoners along its tracks.

The houses were aimed at the middle classes and were carefully controlled in design and number. To own a house in Metro-land was a status symbol. From their windows of leaded diamond panes and their fancifully-illuminated doors incorporating glass that tinged the sun's rays with blues, apple greens and yellows, the fortunate owners looked over a fresh faerie-land, sweet-smelling and very much like the land of Lionel Monckton's Edwardian musical comedies.

Betjeman had been deeply affected as a young boy by Arthur Machen's novel *The Secret Glory*, in which Machen called for a writer 'able to tell the London suburbs the truth about themselves in their own tongue'. Betjeman jumped at the chance to realise this aspiration, and in 1972 collaborated with Edward Mirzoeff to make a film about Metro-land. At a convivial lunch at one of Betjeman's favourite London restaurants, Wheeler's of Soho, the

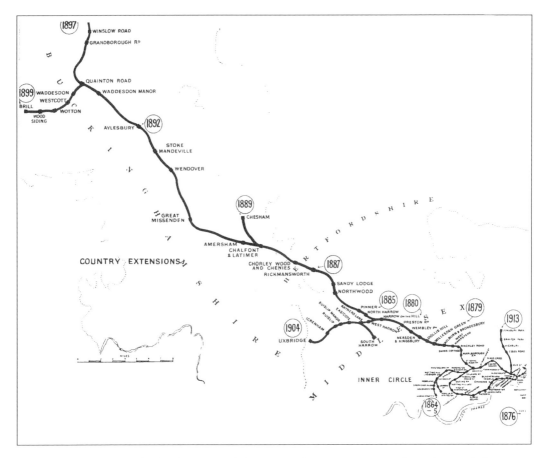

This map shows the early development of the Metropolitan Line in central London, and then the dates of the successive extensions out to Quainton Road and beyond by the end of the nineteenth century.

producer Ted Roberts came up with the idea of travelling along the Metropolitan Line as the spine of the film.

By good luck Michael Robbins, the Managing Director of London Underground, had recently come across an original Metropolitan Railway black-and-white film of 1910 that was taken from the driver's cab of an electric train and showed the countryside around Neasden and Harrow before the housebuilding boom began. This film, sped up, formed the opening sequence, accompanied by the music of 'Tiger Rag' played by the Temperance Seven. Then comes Betjeman's introduction:

Child of the First War, forgotten by the Second,
We called you Metro-land. We laid our schemes lured by the lush brochure, down byways beckoned,
To build at last the cottage of our dreams,
A city clerk turned countryman again,
And linked to the Metropolis by train.

The journey begins beneath Chiltern Court at Baker Street where businessmen's wives lunched in the elegant surroundings of the Chiltern Court Restaurant, and then Betjeman travels out, past the villas of St John's Wood, to Neasden:

> Out of the chimney-pots into the openness,
> Till we come to the suburb that's thought to be commonplace,
> Home of the gnome and the average citizen,
> Sketchley and Unigate, Dolcis and Walpamur.

Then on we travel to Wembley, where Metro-land really begins, and where Sir Edward Watkin, Chairman of the Metropolitan Line, tried and failed to erect his own Eiffel Tower on the site of Wembley Stadium. There is a brief autobiographical flashback to a visit with his father in 1924 to the British Empire Exhibition, and then we continue along the line to Harrow-on-the-Hill, with shots of straw-hatted public school boys, Grim's Dyke (best known as the home of W. S. Gilbert), Pinner with its medieval fair, Moor Park Golf Club, a Wurlitzer organ in a private house in Chorleywood, 'which is, I think, essential Metro-land', and on through the beechwoods of the Chilterns to Amersham:

> In those wet fields the railway didn't pay,
> The Metro stops at Amersham today.

Baker Street station is the main station on the Metropolitan Line, the gateway to Metro-land in one direction and the City in the other. In 1912 the Metropolitan Railway rebranded itself as electric and forward-looking, and created passenger traffic from the housing estates it developed along the line. At Baker Street they built a huge office block – Chiltern Court – above the station, which housed the headquarters and included a smart restaurant for those wanting a meal on their trips up to London. As John Betjeman wrote in his book on London's stations, 'The Metropolitan at Baker Street and its neighbour the Great Central are Edwardian: they go with silk hats, trim beards, cigars, glasses of port and ladies who ... get their furniture from Maples.'

'Gaily into Ruislip Gardens; Runs the red electric train...' Ruislip Gardens station, which opened in 1934 on the Central Line, connecting central London with the newly created suburbs, was immortalised in John Betjeman's poem 'Middlesex', in which he imagines the office girl Elaine getting out of the red electric train and walking to her home in the 'lost Elysium' of rural Middlesex. (Courtesy of Stuart Vallis)

The film ends in the Vale of Aylesbury with Betjeman standing on the bridge at the disused Quainton Road station, which was to have been 'the Clapham Junction of the rural part of the Metropolitan'. He remembers seeing a branch line train waiting to take two or three passengers to Brill, and in the final scene stands leaning on a fence at Verney Junction. Here, with nobody in sight, Betjeman turns to the camera and says, 'The houses of Metro-land never got as far as Verney Junction. Grass triumphs. And I must say I'm rather glad.'

The Brill branch line, mentioned in the film, closed in 1935, with passenger services to Verney Junction in 1936, and after the extension of electric traction to Amersham in 1961 the train services to Aylesbury were taken over by British Railways. Betjeman's commentary, often in iambic pentameters, brought warmth, humour, suspense and insight to the moving images. He rehabilitated at a stroke the status of suburbia as a desirable place to live and reminded us why we could learn to love a railway that linked together the City clerks, the managerial classes who moved into the country estates of Metro-land, and the country gentry who travelled up to town for a couple of days on business or to visit their London clubs.

Norfolk

I first got to know East Anglia as a schoolboy, going on a bicycling holiday through Essex into Suffolk, with a memory of a misty morning at Hadleigh Mill and the lovely church with its fourteenth-century font, stalls, bench ends and brasses. Then it was on to the fine wool church at Lavenham and back via Stoke by Nayland and Colchester and the train to London.

It wasn't until much later, when I was a curate and recently married, that I discovered the delights of north Norfolk, staying for a post-Easter holiday with my wife in a tiny cottage in the village of East Tuddenham, just off the busy main road into Norwich. I remember looking in an estate agent's window and seeing, in 1974, very modestly priced cottages, which were nevertheless beyond my reach on a curate's stipend. Since then house prices in Norfolk have soared, especially on the north Norfolk coast, now

The salt marshes beyond the village of Blakeney are home to many varieties of bird life and offer panoramic views of this wide-open north Norfolk coastline. (Courtesy of Stuart Vallis)

nicknamed 'Chelsea on Sea'. It is not surprising, as the stretch of coastline from Burnham Market to Cromer is a place of beauty and mystery, a paradise for the birdwatcher, the walker, the sailor and the church crawler. Inland there are the splendours of Houghton and Holkham, with villages of brick-and-flint cottages, sometimes clustered into townships such as the Burnhams, or hugging the shores of an estuary as at Cley, Salthouse and Blakeney. And wherever you look in the wide East Anglian sky there are church towers – circular or square – soaring skywards above the trees, surrounded by fields, tying the landscape together in a patchwork of ancient communal belonging and rootedness. Even today it is possible to turn off the busy main roads and travel along quiet lanes to small villages, between tall hedgerows and open farmland, passing few cars and only the occasional cyclist.

This remote part of England, which still jealousy guards its own identity, was opened up in the nineteenth century, both by Edward VII making his country home at Sandringham, and by the arrival of the Midland & Great Northern Railway, which linked Sheringham and Cromer to Norwich. The line is still in use and an extension to Holt is run as the heritage line, the North Norfolk Railway. Railways, churches, quiet countryside and salt sea air – Norfolk remains a golden county. It is no wonder John Betjeman loved it.

*****

In 1973, John Betjeman, by now Poet Laureate and a Knight of the Realm, was invited together with the Bishop of Norwich, the Rt Revd Maurice Wood, to become joint presidents of the Midland and Great Northern Joint Railway Society, the charity that supports the North Norfolk Railway. This operates a 5.25-mile heritage railway from Sheringham to Holt in north Norfolk, and had been founded in 1959. This appointment happily brought together two of Betjeman's passions, steam trains and the East Anglian countryside, which he had known since boyhood. He had first visited Norfolk with his father, sailing on the Norfolk Broads. His imagination had also been kindled by hearing *Ghost Stories of an Antiquary* by M. R. James read to him as a boy at the Dragon School in Oxford. He felt that these tales 'bring out the

Above left: John Betjeman was invited to become president of the Midland & Great Northern Joint Railway Society, which runs the North Norfolk Railway, a heritage line that runs from Sheringham to Holt. Here John Betjeman could indulge his love of steam trains as they puff along the coast to the terminus at Holt. (Courtesy of Stuart Vallis)

Above right: No. 92203 *Black Prince* prepares to depart from Holt station, with driver and fireman at the ready. (Courtesy of Stuart Vallis)

Above left: It could be a scene from the 1940s, but is in fact a summer's day in 2019 at Holt station, north Norfolk. (Courtesy of Stuart Vallis)

Above right: The 1940s comes to Holt. A policeman in authentic wartime uniform stands at his post. John Betjeman would have remembered such scenes and been delighted at this modern re-enactment. (Courtesy of Stuart Vallis)

Norfolk landscape, Perpendicular churches, Georgian squire's houses in red brick, Strawberry Hill Gothic, mezzotints and the eighteenth century, as well as the Middle Ages'.

For Betjeman, memories of Norfolk were freighted not just with nostalgia, but also with guilt. It was to Norfolk that his father had taken him as a boy when their relationship was still in good heart. Together they had gone to the Norfolk Broads on sailing holidays and he remembered a day, when he was eight or nine years old with his father on the River Bure, when they passed the tower of Belaugh Church: 'It was the outline of that church tower of Belaugh against the sky that gave me a passion for churches.' He dated his lifelong love of church crawling to that moment. But he also spent his honeymoon with Penelope, the daughter of Lord and Lady Chetwode, bicycling around Norfolk, and those memories too will have stirred up the guilt he felt at the breakdown of their relationship and his conflicted love life. In spite of such uncomfortable feelings, Norfolk was chosen for his next major TV film and the view of Belaugh from the River Bure became part of the opening sequence.

After the success of *Metro-Land* in 1973, there was great enthusiasm for a follow-up film, and Eddie Mirzoeff felt that a film about the Church of England would both break new ground and appeal to Betjeman. He was right, and filming began in April 1974. After some hesitation, and with the blessing of Maurice Wood, Bishop of Norwich, East Anglia and the diocese of Norwich was chosen for a film about the life of Betjeman's beloved Church of England. By good luck and hard work the characters, vignettes and settings appeared and took shape: a montage of Norfolk churches, including the cathedral-like Cley-next-the-Sea; the roof at Knapton; the rood screens at Ranworth and Great Snoring; the fifteenth-century glass at Warham in an unspoilt eighteenth-century interior; a baptism in the font at Trunch, with its splendid canopy of around *c.* 1500; the Rector of Weston Longville putting together his parish magazine; the PCC meeting; the visit to Felbrigg Church where Betjeman found visitors rubbing the medieval brass of Sir Symon Felbrigge and his wife, showing them side by side, linking nicely to a contemporary wedding at Lyng; then on to the Anglican Shrine to Our Lady at Walsingham; then Sandringham; J. N. Comper's work at Wymondham Abbey; the missions to seamen chaplain at Great Yarmouth and the chaplain to the Norfolk

John Betjeman's writing was influenced by wartime patriotism and the desire to record and celebrate the beauty of England as a reminder of what the nation was fighting for. (Courtesy of Stuart Vallis)

When John Piper became involved in the *Shell Guides* he liked the idea of a sketchbook as a working format, with found illustrations and small drawings and photographs. In his 1969 revision of the *Norfolk Guide* he included a number of drawings by the Norfolk artist and antiquary John Sell Cotman (1782–1842) because of the romantic atmosphere of pleasing decay that they evoked. This shows 'The Late Vicarage House, Methwould.'

Above: St Margaret's, Cley-next-the-Sea. The church was magnificently rebuilt in the fourteenth and fifteenth centuries, the transepts left in ruins since the sixteenth century. (Courtesy of Stuart Vallis)

Left: The splendid change to fifteenth-century porch, ashlar faced and two-storied, with niches, shields and traceried windows, of St Margaret's, Cley. (Courtesy of Stuart Vallis)

Above left: South porch, Cley. The Perpendicular vaulted porch entrance, with a Decorated south doorway and ancient door. (Courtesy of Stuart Vallis)

Above right: A total of 138 angels guard the worshippers at Knapton church, supporting one of the finest double hammer-beam roofs in East Anglia. (Courtesy of Stuart Vallis)

Right: St Peter and St Paul's Church, Knapton. High up in the roof, and hard to see with the human eye, this angel pipes her heavenly music and looks down on the worshippers below. She has been doing so since 1504. (Courtesy of Stuart Vallis)

Broads; and the climax of the film, Easter Day at Ness Point, Lowestoft, with an inevitable poetic reference to the church bells of St Peter Mancroft in Norwich.

> Across the diocese from tower to tower
> The church bells exercise compelling power.
> 'Come all to church, good people,' hear them say;
> 'Come all to church, today is Easter Day'.

Above left: The ancient south door at All Saints Church, Bale, studded with old ironwork and set in a simple pointed arch has welcomed countless visitors and worshippers over the centuries. (Courtesy of Stuart Vallis)

Above right: All Saints, Bale. In a window in the nave is a fine collection of medieval glass, including this representation of the Annunciation from the fifteenth century. (Courtesy of Stuart Vallis)

Below: Founded in the eleventh century by Benedictine monks, not much remains of Binham Priory except the nave of the church. (Courtesy of Stuart Vallis)

The fine west front of Binham Priory, *c.* 1240. The window was bricked up when building activity came to an end. It is an active parish church and guests at a wedding mingle happily under the dog-tooth mouldings of the doorway. (Courtesy of Stuart Vallis)

Above: St Nicholas' Church, Blakeney. Inside, sunlight streams into this large and airy church and falls on ancient misericords in the chancel. (Courtesy of Stuart Vallis)

Right: The evening sun lights up the slender tower at the north-east corner of Blakeney Church, which perkily competes with the impressive bulk of the west tower. Surely it was originally some kind of beacon to guide ships into Blakeney Harbour. (Courtesy of Stuart Vallis)

Above left: In the middle of a beautiful park landscaped by Humphrey Repton and overlooked by Felbrigg Hall stands St Margaret's Church, approached only by footpaths and surrounded by a grove of trees. Inside there is a fine series of brasses, including the memorial to Sir Symon Felbrigge and Margaret, his first wife (1416), showing them beneath a double canopy. He was standard-bearer to Richard II and is depicted as a Knight of the Garter. When filming for *A Passion for Churches* John Betjeman found this brass being rubbed – 'the new cottage industry'. (Courtesy of Stuart Vallis)

Above right: St Margaret's Church, Felbrigg. In the chancel the fine monument to the statesman William Windham (1750–1810) by Joseph Nollekens was stuck unceremoniously against the beautiful Perpendicular sedilia. He is described on his memorial as 'frank, generous, unassuming, intrepid, compassionate and pious'. (Courtesy of Stuart Vallis)

Although the film's title *A Passion for Churches* suggests it is going to be a church crawl with Sir John, in fact it uses individual churches and people to reveal the life, breadth and character of the Church of England. Betjeman was adamant that the film should not be overtly religious or proselytising. It should take for granted that the Church of England was the national church, always there, and show its immense variety, warm humanity, good humour and everyday spiritual life, all through the prism of a particular diocese – Norwich. The film succeeds, again because Betjeman married his commentary very effectively to the film's images, so bringing out his underlying message, which he sums up in the final two lines:

And though for church we may not seem to care,
It's deeply part of us. Thank God it's there.

The fifteenth-century screen at St Mary's Church, Great Snoring, frames the chancel and adds a sense of prayerful mystery to this modest church. (Courtesy of Stuart Vallis)

Above left: St Mary's Church, Great Snoring. This painted panel on the rood screen shows the Blessed Virgin Mary wearing a red mantle, carrying the Christ child, and holding three red roses. (Courtesy of Stuart Vallis)

Above right: St Botolph's, Trunch, another church visited by John Betjeman when filming *A Passion for Churches*. Its glory is the extraordinary font canopy dating from the fifteenth century, one of only four in England. It has two parts: the lower canopy on posts with a fan-vaulted ceiling, and the upper part with eight hanging vaulted canopies. You feel that babies baptised in this font will have been welcomed into the church with all due ceremony. (Courtesy of Stuart Vallis)

Above left: During the late nineteenth and into the twentieth century, St Mary's, Warham, fell into disuse. It was rescued through the efforts of Wilhelmine, Lady Harrod, a friend of John Betjeman, who worked tirelessly to save the medieval churches of Norfolk that were threatened with demolition. Her monument is placed on the south wall of the nave. (Courtesy of Stuart Vallis)

Above right: St Mary's Church, Warham, a chapel of ease set behind a wall and iron gates with a Gothic south door. It is dusty and cobwebby inside, but has an unspoilt eighteenth-century interior with box pews and a triple-decker pulpit – just what John Betjeman loved. (Courtesy of Stuart Vallis)

Left: St Mary's, Warham, has a rich collection of fourteenth- and fifteenth-century Norwich glass. Here a mischievous-looking angel swings a censer. (Courtesy of Stuart Vallis)

St Mary's, Warham. A
fifteenth-century priest with
wonderfully curly hair looks
reflectively at us across the
centuries. (Courtesy of Stuart
Vallis)

An angel playing a lute at
St Mary's, Warham. (Courtesy
of Stuart Vallis)

5

Eternity Contained in Time...

I was brought up in the Presbyterian Church in England, and so I only came to experience Anglicanism in my late teens when I went up to Oxford University and took an active part in the worship in chapel at Oriel College. In the late 1960s the Book of Common Prayer was still the service book in regular use, and I was drawn to its austere spirituality and sublime language, especially in the context of the seventeenth-century, wood-panelled chapel with its simple altar, silver candlesticks and splendid brass candelabra with candles ablaze for choral evensong. When I started to study theology as part of my ordination training, I spent a year living in Pusey House on St Giles in Oxford, founded in 1884 as a lay community of piety and learning and presided over by a principal, librarian and chaplain, all ordained clergymen in the Anglo-Catholic tradition.

The house was full of interesting and odd characters, and a congenial place in which to reside while studying, with its communal meals, ecclesiastical library and soaring chapel

Pusey House Chapel, St Giles, Oxford. Founded in 1884 by Charles Gore as a memorial to Edward Bouverie Pusey, it was designed by the architect Temple Moore in a neo-Gothic style and completed in 1914.

designed by Temple Moore with a fine altar and baldachino by Ninian Comper, where daily Mass was celebrated, and High Mass on Sundays. Just as John Betjeman before me, through the combination of Anglo-Catholic ceremonial and lusty congregational hymn singing I found my faith deepened and enlarged. I embraced the traditions that the Oxford Movement and the ritualist pioneers had revived and kept alive within the Church of England, and through these and other influences found myself drawn gently but surely towards the priesthood. Since then I have served in town parishes, rural parishes and latterly in the City of London at St Bride's Church, Fleet Street. At St Bride's the rectory was tucked away behind Wren's magnificent church, with its 'wedding-cake' spire, and so for fourteen years I lived in the heart of London, in an area that still holds traces of its medieval street pattern and of the coffee house culture of Samuel Richardson and Dr Johnson. The big newspaper groups had mostly moved away to other parts of the metropolis, but there were still a few news agencies left, and journalists always enjoyed coming back for memorial services for old comrades and a chance for a drink in El Vino's. This was the area that Betjeman would have known in its heyday when he was himself a journalist. Further down towards the Strand was the Temple, with its Inns of Court, Dickensian alleyways and atmosphere and the Round Church built in imitation of the Holy Sepulchre in Jerusalem, with Templar Knights recumbent on the floor. In the other direction loomed the mighty dome of St Paul's Cathedral at the top of Ludgate Hill, and the churches, financial institutions, livery halls and hidden corners of the City of London, 'the many-steepled London Sky' so dear to John Betjeman.

Now, in retirement, I have left the crowded streets of London behind and settled in Oxford, the city of my birth. The wheel has come full circle, and I have been able to reconnect with both the city and University of Oxford, and with the Cotswold countryside to which my parents introduced me over sixty years ago. The constant thread running through my life from boyhood has been a fascination with the built environment, especially with the parish churches of England, but in later years also with Victorian and Edwardian art and architecture. Whenever I enter a church, I am aware not just of the architectural details, but also the place memories of all those who have worshipped and prayed in that building – their lives, loves, hopes and fears – and because of that I feel strengthened to cope with my own insecurities and longings. In that sense every church is, in Philip Larkin's memorable phrase, 'a serious house on serious earth ... in whose blent air all our compulsions meet, are recognised and robed as destinies...' It is because of that underlying spiritual resonance, so deeply felt by Betjeman, that these 'liminal places', 'Eternity contained in time...' in the poet's words, should be treasured, conserved, used and embraced by every generation.

*****

By the mid-1970s John Betjeman was clearly showing the effects of the Parkinson's disease that blighted his last decade. His shuffling gait and lack of balance made film work more problematic, but he still took part in Jonathan Stedall's TV film of his autobiographical *Summoned by Bells* in 1976. He found the filming emotionally draining because he had to delve back into his earliest memories and experiences. He said he felt as though he were undressing in public. Jonathan Stedall remembers those days of filming on location with fondness. Betjeman always made filming fun, and he knew instinctively when images

Daymer Bay, Trebetherick, Cornwall. (Courtesy of Stuart Vallis)

could speak for themselves, with no need for words. He loved to imagine the lives of those who lived or worked in the buildings and places where they filmed, and his sense of intimacy with the viewer, and his enthusiasm, were enticing and contagious.

Even more remarkably, considering the progress of his Parkinson's, in 1981 and 1982 Betjeman made another TV series with Jonathan Stedall called *Time with Betjeman*. Clips from Betjeman's earlier broadcasts were interwoven with conversations about his life and beliefs. It was an extraordinarily intimate and moving portrait, which revealed the essence of the man, with his defences down. Now an old and ailing man, Betjeman had become more open, more distrustful of certainties and more humble, content to look and listen rather than always being the performer. At the end of the film, after one of many pauses, Betjeman is gazing out to sea, happy and peaceful. Finally, he murmurs: 'Eternity is around us all the time.' When the film was shown on television there were voices raised in protest, but in a way the film was only celebrating what Betjeman had been happy to do all his life, that is to reveal himself, his life, his loves and beliefs through his poetry, prose and broadcasting. He seemed comfortable giving expression to the development of his inner life and sharing his passions and his fears with the world. Indeed, that had always been one of his strengths – the willingness to make himself vulnerable through the sharing of himself openly and candidly.

The author Susan Hill, in an article written just after Betjeman's death in 1984, wrote:

By giving us so much of himself, so many intimate details of his own life, his childhood memories, his fears, loves, obsessions, beliefs, by being so utterly truthful, John Betjeman does far more than simply tell us those things. He helps us to see our own selves, to learn about our pasts, and the places and people in them, to reveal what is important about our own experiences.

John Betjeman's final years were a burden to him, but the stream of letters from the public kept pouring in and so, with the assistance of a couple of secretaries, he answered them.

Archibald Ormsby-Gore, John Betjeman's beloved teddy bear, his companion from childhood until death. (Courtesy of Stuart Vallis)

In May 1984 he went down to Cornwall, to Trebetherick, the place that held so many memories and where he was happiest. He died peacefully there on the morning of 19 May, surrounded by those who cared for him and holding his beloved teddy bear Archie. The funeral took place a few days later at St Enodoc in suitably stormy Cornish weather. He is buried in the churchyard there, the grave marked by a stone of Cornish Delabole slate with elaborate flourished lettering by Simon Verity.

Betjeman prided himself on being self-taught, not 'an expert' or a professional architectural historian. He revelled in eccentricity and was fond of unearthing the unconventional and unregarded among people, buildings and literature. He had a powerful visual sense and the ability to express that in words. The war years realigned and refocused his vision of England away from modernism towards a romantic love of the vernacular, the picturesque and the enduring elements of English life and character, stimulated by his friendship with John Piper. In a number of essays he summed up what England meant to him and to many of his generation who endured the trauma and uncertainty of the Second World War. In his radio broadcast of February 1943 called *Coming Home, or England Revisited*, he said:

> For me, England stands for the Church of England, eccentric incumbents, oil-lit churches, Women's Institutes, modest village inns, the noise of mowing machines on Saturday afternoons, local newspapers, the poetry of Tennyson, Crabbe, Hardy and Matthew Arnold, a visit to the cinema, branch-line trains, leaning on gates and looking across fields.

If that list sounds impossibly romantic, nostalgic and unreal it is worth remembering that this was Betjeman's personal response at a time when Britain was facing the potential destruction of her way of life at the hands of Nazi Germany, and so he was entitled to feel romantic and nostalgic. Later on, in an article in the *Spectator* for 29 October 1954, Betjeman made a brief but spirited defence of a nostalgic approach to life. He said, 'Nostalgic ... is a scientific word for "sentimental" and sounds like a form of catarrh. I regard 'nostalgic' as a term of praise myself, for it implies reverence and a sense of the past and an awareness of, though not necessarily slavery to tradition.' John Piper, too, said of Betjeman: 'He taught me how to be nostalgic without being sentimental.'

What mattered to Betjeman were the people and the buildings and the institutions that gave a sense of depth and continuity and fun to the nation's life, the pastoral landscape of England, the thousands of modest, unspoilt places in these islands, the spiritual dimension to human existence that he felt was increasingly being neglected. By his writing and broadcasting he wanted to shake English people out of their spiritual and cultural indifference. Above all he wanted to communicate his love of buildings and places to people who rarely read architectural books but did visit and use the churches, railway stations and the streetscapes and countryside of England. He wanted them to 'see' as he did, to share his perception of the mystery and beauty and eccentricity that are all around us if only we will look and observe.

In another article written by Susan Hill in the months after John Betjeman's death on 19 May 1984, she describes coming across a photograph of her daughter standing beside Betjeman's grave in the churchyard of St Enodoc at Trebetherick in his beloved Cornwall, and reflecting on what he had meant to her: 'As I stood, looking down at the grave, I thought a great many thoughts about Sir John Betjeman, and about myself, my own life, and his influence and impact upon me, realising, perhaps for the first time, how tremendous it has been.'

In his own lifetime he profoundly influenced the way we look at our surroundings. He created his own attitude and became the embodiment of that attitude, and by sharing so much of his inner life, his beliefs and passions, hopes and fears, he encouraged us to look afresh at our own histories, to catch his own enthusiasm, and move from being mere spectators to being engaged participants, to respond with eye and ear and heart as we interact with the built environment and seek to hand it on enhanced, not diminished, to future generations.

Sir John Betjeman's memorial service in Westminster Abbey concluded with Canon Trevor Beeson reading the beautiful prayer by John Donne (1572–1631), Dean of St Paul's Cathedral, London:

BRING us, O Lord, at our last awakening into the house and gate of heaven, to enter into that gate and dwell in that house, where there shall be no darkness nor dazzling but one equal light, no noise nor silence but one equal music, no fears nor hopes

John Betjeman in characteristic pose, gazing at one of his favourite Cornish churches (St Protus and St Hyacinth, Blisland) and finding the eternal in the present moment. (Courtesy of Jonathan Stedall)

Sunset over the medieval bridge at Wadebridge, Cornwall. (Courtesy of Stuart Vallis)

but one equal possession, no ends nor beginnings, but one equal eternity, in the habitations of thy majesty and thy glory, world without end. *Amen.*

John Betjeman understood that familiar things and places invite us on a voyage of discovery, and he saw our world as a place of unforeseen wonder and mystery, pointing beyond itself to eternal habitations and a glory yet to be revealed. It seems an appropriate prayer with which to crown his life and legacy.

St Protus and St Hyacinth, Blisland. A stone ledger slab in the north chapel floor, calling passers-by to remember their own mortality. (Courtesy of Stuart Vallis)

Behold and see our natures frame
Returned to dust from whence it came
Hold fast by Christ which lead the way
Our souls to heaven to convey.

APPENDIX ONE

Chronology of John Betjeman's Life

1906	Born at Highgate, London, 28 August
1917	Dragon School, Oxford
1920	Marlborough College, Wiltshire
1925	Magdalene College, Oxford
1928	Schoolmaster at Thorpe House Preparatory School, Gerrards Cross
1929–30	Schoolmaster at Heddon Court Preparatory School, East Barnet
1930–34	Assistant Editor, *Architectural Review*
1932	Beginning of the *Shell Guides* series
1933	Publication of *Ghastly Good Taste*
	Marries Penelope Chetwode
1934	Move to Garrards Farm, Uffington, Berkshire, and publication of *Cornwall*
1936	*Shell Guide to Devon*
1937	*Continual Dew*
1938	*An Oxford University Chest*
1940	*Old Lights for New Chancels*
1941	UK press attaché in Dublin
1943	*English Cities and Small Towns*
1945	Move to Farnborough, Berkshire
1948	*Selected Poems*
	Murray's Buckinghamshire Architectural Guide
1949	*Murray's Berkshire Architectural Guide*
1950	*Collected Poems*
1951	Move to The Mead, Wantage, Berkshire
	Shell Guide to Shropshire, published in collaboration with John Piper
1954	Rents No. 43 Cloth Fair, City of London
	A Few Late Chrysanthemums
1955	*Discovering Britain* films for Shell
1956	*The English Town in the Last One Hundred Years*
1958	*Collins Guide to English Parish Churches*
	Collected Poems

1960	*Summoned by Bells*
	Queen's Gold Medal for Poetry
	Appointed CBE
	Buys Treen at Trebetherick, Cornwall
1960–68	*ABC of Churches* films for the BBC
1961	Euston Arch and Great Hall demolished
1965	*The City of London Churches*
1966	*High and Low*
1969	*Victorian and Edwardian London*
1972	*London's Historic Railway Stations*
	A Pictorial History of English Architecture
1973	*Metro-Land* film for BBC
	Rents No. 29 Radnor Walk, Chelsea, London
1974	*A Passion for Churches,* film for the BBC
1976	*Summoned by Bells,* film for the BBC
	Vicar of This Parish: Betjeman on Kilvert, film for the BBC
1978	*The Best of Betjeman*
1980	*Church Poems*
1982	*Uncollected Poems*
1983	*Time with Betjeman* films for the BBC
1984	Dies, Trebetherick, 19 May

Some Favourite Betjeman Churches

This list is partial and selective, but it aims to highlight some of John Betjeman's favourite churches and places for those who wish to explore further with a Betjemanesque eye for detail. Visit not just for the church, but for the village or urban context and the other fine buildings among which the church is set.

Bedfordshire	Elstow – St Mary and St Helen
Berkshire	Compton Beauchamp – St Swithin
	Shottesbrooke – St John the Baptist
	Uffington – Assumption of the BVM
Bristol:	Bristol – St Mary Redcliffe
Buckinghamshire	Nether Winchendon – St Nicholas
	Thornton St Michael
Cambridgeshire	Westerley Waterless – St Mary the Less
Cornwall	Blisland – St Probus & St Hyacinth
	St Endellion – St Endelienta
	St Enodoc
Devon	Dartmouth – St Petroc
	Ottery St Mary – St Mary
Dorset:	Lytchett Matravers – St Mary
	Whitchurch Canonicorum – St Candida & Holy Cross
Essex	Thaxted – St John, St Mary & St Laurence

Gloucestershire	Fairford – St Mary the Virgin
	Northleach – St Peter & St Paul
Herefordshire	Monnington-on-Wye – St Mary the Virgin
	Shobdon – St John the Evangelist
Kent	Chilham – St Mary
	Kemsing – St Mary
	Upper Hardres – St Peter & St Paul
Lincolnshire	Bag Enderby – St Margaret
	Silk Willoughby – St Denis
	Stamford – All Saints, St George's, St John's, St Mary's
	Tattershall – Holy Trinity
London	St Bartholomew-the-Great
	St Cyprian's, Clarence Gate
	St Mary Magdalene, Paddington
	St Mary-le-Strand
	St Stephen Walbrook
Middlesex	Harefield – St Mary
	Harmondsworth: Tithe Barn
	Harrow-on-the-Hill – St Mary
Norfolk	Cley-next-the-Sea – St Margaret
	Felbrigg St Margaret
	Holkham – St Witburga
	Salle – St Peter & St Paul
	Trunch – St Botolph
Northamptonshire	Cottesbrooke – All Saints
	Wellingborough – St Mary
Oxfordshire	Burford – St John the Baptist
	Ewelme – St Mary the Virgin
	Oxford – St Barnabas
Pusey House	
	Waterperry – St Mary the Virgin
	Widford – St Oswald
Rutland	Ketton – St Mary
	Tixover – St Luke

Somerset	Batcombe – St Mary
	Cricket Malherbie – St Mary Magdalene
	Mells – St Andrew
Suffolk	Blythburgh – Holy Trinity
	Lavenham – St Peter & St Paul
	Long Melford – Holy Trinity
	Stoke by Nayland – St Mary
Surrey:	Albury – St Peter & St Paul
	Hascombe – St Peter
	Lingfield – St Peter & St Paul
Sussex:	Amberley – St Michael
	Brighton – St Bartholomew
	Rye – St Mary
Warwickshire	Hampton Lucy – St Peter ad Vincular
	Wilmcote – St Andrew
Wiltshire	Bishopstone, S. Wilts – St John the Baptist
	Boscombe – St Andrew
	Dilton – St Mary
	Steeple Ashton – St Mary the Virgin
	Winterbourne Bassett – St Kathrine & St Peter
Worcestershire	Bredon – St Giles
	Broadway – St Eadburgh
Yorkshire	Baldersby – St James
	Beverley – St John of Beverley, St Mary
	Cowthorpe – St Michael
	Easby – St Agatha
	Grinton – St Andrew
	Harrogate – St Wilfred
	Lastingham – St Mary
	Patrington – St Patrick
	Selby – St Mary & St Germaine
	Studley Royal – St Mary the Virgin
	Wensley – Holy Trinity
	Wintringham – St Peter